GREAT
RACES,
INCREDIBLE
PLACES

A street sign in Bhutan

GREAT RACES, INCREDIBLE PLACES

100+ FANTASTIC RUNS AROUND THE WORLD

KIMI PUNTILLO

BANTAM BOOKS

GREAT RACES, INCREDIBLE PLACES
A Bantam Book / April 2009

Published by Bantam Dell
A Division of Random House, Inc.
New York, New York

Book design by Helene Berinsky

Library of Congress Cataloging-in-Publication Data
Puntillo, Kimi.
    Great races, incredible places : 100+ fantastic runs around the world /
Kimi Puntillo.
        p. cm.
    ISBN 978-0-553-38532-8 (trade pbk.)
    1. Running races—Guidebooks.   2. Long-distance running—Guidebooks.
    I. Title.
    GV1061.P86 2009
    796.42—dc22   2008041395

Printed in the United States of America
Published simultaneously in Canada

www.bantamdell.com

BVG   10 9 8 7 6 5 4 3 2 1

To Helen,
who never gives up on love or a commitment,
and Mike,
who never gives up on enjoying life

An Important Note to Readers

While every effort has been made to accurately depict the context and conditions of each of these notable races, they are subject to unexpected change due to economic, political, or natural forces. Readers should be sure to confirm all pertinent information provided in this text before making travel arrangements or other race-related commitments.

Participation in races found in this book involves inherent risks, both known and unknown or unforeseeable at the present time, including personal and bodily injury and property loss or damage. The author, editors, and publisher shall not be responsible for injuries incurred by the reader while participating in any of the races described in this book. All readers electing to participate in any of the races mentioned should be sure that they meet the required health and physical standards to compete. In addition, they should be sure to take every precaution to protect their person as befits the conditions and circumstances surrounding each individual race.

If you discover any out-of-date or incorrect information we would appreciate it if you would bring it to our attention via e-mail at info@GreatRaces-IncrediblePlaces.com.

There are no shortcuts
to any place worth going.

—ANONYMOUS

Acknowledgments

It's been a long journey since my first marathon, with many people to thank along the way. In addition to those who helped me with my book, there are numerous friends, family, and loved ones who supported me through my worldwide adventures. Some were complete strangers who showed a little kindness, still remembered; others I was fortunate enough to keep as friends.

For the kindred spirits who opened their homes and hearts to me, I thank you for easing my way on the road and through other obstacles. My love to those who supported me on the sidelines at my first New York City Marathon: Mom and Dad, and Alice. Warm wishes go out to friends who kept me company when I was far from home. Steven was at the finish line of the Buenos Aires Maratón Adidas, when I became the first woman to run a marathon on every continent in the world. Melanie also traveled far to greet me at a race.

My sister, Michelle, stood with a baby carriage holding my precious goddaughter, Michaela, at a deserted Logan International Airport, in Boston. I had finally returned to the U.S., after boarding a plane on September 11, 2001, following the Marathon du Médoc, in France. Caring thoughts go to Charlotte and others familiar with my love of travel, who called to make sure I was all right.

Running buddies were essential, the best being my yellow lab, Beethoven, who was always ready to go with a smile. (I encourage short runs on cool days, off-leash and off-pavement.) Auntie Lee lovingly translated interviews with Italian race directors. Sister Judith took the time to offer kind words of encouragement, while Robin and Phil were supportive friends.

Thanks to Toby for rallying the troops when needed. Mark and Melina were consistently gracious hosts, as was Mark Tully. And many thanks to Deborah, who alleviated a multitude of aches and pains, and helped ignite my journeys when she said, "There's this marathon in Antarctica that I'm thinking of doing."

Assistance was important in researching this book. Thank you, Michelle Stockman, for your dependability and amazing knowledge of technology. Renee Leck provided unwavering support and much appreciated flexibility on the home stretch. Stacey Bond "took the hill" when asked a research question and never came back empty-handed. And to Peter Allen, a good neighbor and ace photojournalist, who was always ready to contribute. Yuya's creative eye was valued, as was input from Kelsey, Carly, Matt, Laura, Sarah, and Grace.

Ryan Lamppa, at Running USA, was ever so helpful in San Diego. Thank you to all those who took the time to be interviewed, including race directors and runners all around the world. Finally, special thanks to Philip Rappaport and Sharon Propson at Bantam Dell, who went to the mat for the book on several occasions, as did Molly Glick and Jennifer Weltz, my agents.

Contents

GO RUN THE WORLD

What really keeps me lacing up my sneakers day after day is the promise of travel and adventure. Exploring was always a favorite pastime of mine, but I didn't know that running could enhance my trip.

Discovering back roads and beautiful places by foot was a surprising but appreciated reward when I prepared for my first long-distance race, the New York City Marathon. As mileage on the training schedule increased, I welcomed the fresh energy I drew from running by red and yellow foliage, or on urban excursions, past city life that I normally missed while riding public transportation. Combining entertaining routes with the physical and emotional highs that come from mastering long mileage, running became more essential than my morning cup of coffee.

Still, I hadn't planned on running anything beyond my first marathon. Then, I heard about a race in Antarctica. Fulfilling fantasies of witnessing firsthand the majestic, sky blue, multistory icebergs that I had seen in *National Geographic* photographs as a child, I signed up for the second ever Antarctica Marathon. Not only did it fulfill my decades-old dream, it changed my life.

Combining running with travel, I pursued beautiful and unusual races across the U.S. and all over the world, from 5Ks to 26.2-mile marathons. Unexpected surprises unfolded. At the Everest Marathon, I sang with sherpas while camping out at an altitude of 17,000 feet in Nepal. On Cape Cod, a tugboat ferried me along the coast to the start of a 7-mile race on a magnificent summer day. I even traversed 14 miles of jagged lava rock spewed by Kilauea, an active volcano, on the Big Island in Hawaii, in a race that has since been cancelled due to ongoing eruptions of volcanic gases. Finding my footing scaling ice on a glacier, surrounding myself with the rich hues of red rock country, or mastering crumbling steps on the Great Wall of China kept my running fresh. New, remarkable race courses transformed my soles.

Ultimately, I ran a marathon on every continent in the world, earning citations in the *Guinness Book of World Records*. But I'd do it all over again even if someone told me there'd be no records or medals. Running around beautiful places was sheer pleasure. Spending hours outdoors proved an amazing way to enjoy my free time. I accrued enough mileage training and racing to literally run around the circumference of the world.

At races in far-off places, I formed friendships with people I would have never met otherwise, save for planting our sneakers on unique ground. Locals and traveling companions shared stories about their culture, customs, and lives. In an age where globalization creates more misunderstandings than community, running brings people together, creating a strong bond.

My worldwide adventures built an international network of friends over the years, providing memories for more than a lifetime. Sharing these races, and those my friends found spectacular, built the foundation for the collection of runs that you are about to read and consider for yourself.

Imagine finding yourself on a 3-day sail past icebergs in Drake Passage on your way to Antarctica. Wouldn't it be fun to turn back the clock to college road-trip days by gathering eleven buddies and packing them into a van for an overnight relay race? Courses described inside this book will inspire you to broaden your field of dreams and clock additional mileage on your sneakers. New running experiences await you, whether they are halfway around the world, across the country, or in a neighboring community.

You may be tempted to try one, or two, or twenty of these races. Or, you may simply find them entertaining enough to read about and share with a friend who runs or is thinking about becoming a runner. These unique races can motivate even those who don't regularly wear out their sneakers to start exercising in an entertaining new way.

Short or long distances, fun runs with costumes, or long runs that midway through you wonder why you started, there's a race described in this book for every mood and ability. And if you find there's a race that you wish was included, you can spread the word and share it with others by e-mailing info@GreatRaces-IncrediblePlaces.com.

"BECAUSE IT'S THERE"

George Mallory, the British mountaineer, made this phrase famous when questioned why he attempted the daunting feat of climbing Mount Everest. (It took another 29 years before Sir Edmund Hillary made the first successful summit in 1953.) You may find yourself uttering the same response when asked what in the world inspired you to run one of the races described in this section.

Whether you are sailing through the most turbulent body of water in the world, fending off hypothermia in sub-zero temperatures, or scaling rocks above tree lines, these races will test your endurance. Although they sound exhilarating, don't take these adventures lightly. They require serious training to perform your best and help avoid disasters.

Competitors preparing for adventure races have gone to extremes, both in effort and creativity, to simulate course conditions that they'll be encountering. For subfreezing marathons, contenders have gone as far as putting treadmills in industrial walk-in meat lockers. Waterlogged courses have inspired people to train by running through streams.

Race directors can provide essential information on preparing for intense environments that they've selected for their event. Additional details from doctors and other professionals should be sought accordingly. Before the Antarctica Marathon, I learned that it's common for ships to face huge swells sailing across Drake Passage. Speaking at length with my doctors about seasickness, I found the best preventatives suitable for my personal needs. For high altitude courses, I sought advice from specialists who published studies in medical journals on the physical effects and dangers of acclimatizing.

Appropriate, technically correct gear is also vital. Whatever sneakers, leggings, and tops are comfortable on your routine run may not transfer to severely cold temperatures, even if you add layers. Although layering is important to retain body heat, it's just as imperative to plan for it to escape in a timely manner during the race. Otherwise, you may find a sweaty, wet layer that may eventually freeze, sticking to your skin for miles.

Quality gear varies greatly, even when comparing well-known brands. Different skin types can favor one wicking or insulating fabric over another because the fibers of various patented materials such as Polartec® or COOLMAX® have different thread patterns and textures. Trail-running shoes instead of your trusted road-running sneaker may be more suitable for the course, requiring you train in entirely different footwear. Your best bet is to test out gear, subjecting it to the mileage and weather it will endure, well before arriving at the race start.

Researching and preventing potential pitfalls makes all the difference during your adventure race. It also provides perspective on whether you're cut out for an inherently unpredictable trip, or would prefer a race that's more conventional.

If you are up for the challenge, take your pick among these Incredible Races and devote time to research and train for the extreme conditions. Then, get ready for a once-in-a-lifetime experience that you'll be asked to recount over and over again the minute you cross the finish line.

ANTARCTICA MARATHON & HALF-MARATHON
The Lost Continent

LOCATION: KING GEORGE ISLAND, ANTARCTICA

MONTH: FEBRUARY/MARCH

DISTANCE/AVERAGE FIELD: 26.2 MILES/120, 13.1 MILES/30

TELEPHONE: 617-242-7845

WEBSITE: www.marathontours.com/antarctica

How do you get to the bottom of the world to run the Antarctica Marathon? It's not easy. First, you fly to Buenos Aires, Argentina, and then to Ushuaia, on the tip of South America. Ushuaia's claim to fame is that it's the southernmost city in the world, although it more closely resembles a large town. Here you board refitted ships, ice class rated and reinforced with steel hulls to dodge icebergs. Once used for polar research, now the vessels accommodate adventurous runners setting sail for a three-day journey across Drake Passage, the most turbulent body of water in the world.

Pray for tolerable swells. Waves have swept over the deck on rough days, rocking and rolling the boat, so that no amount of Dramamine® could provide relief from the inevitable seasickness. One participant lamented that had he known how brutal the return trip would be, he would have stayed on the "lost continent." The small ship is home for the next week and a half because there's no place to stay or eat in Antarctica. Thousands of miles from civilization, the mainland has no hotels, restaurants, or stores.

King George Island, located off the Antarctic Peninsula, is where you'll join the select club of marathon and half-marathon runners lucky enough to race on the last-discovered continent. First sighted around 1820, the question of whether it was found by an American, Englishman, or Russian is still under debate. On a map, the Antarctic Peninsula looks similar to an arm reaching north, like a straightened Cape Cod.

Once you arrive, stepping onto land where only a tiny fraction of the world's population has left a footprint is breathtaking. The unique feeling is much like holding a newborn child.

On race day, runners bundled in cold-weather gear are shuttled to shore by inflated-rubber Zodiac boats. I stored sneakers and postrace clothes in garbage bags to protect them from ocean spray breaking over the bow. The only sign of human life ashore is several small groupings of trailers, occupied by researchers from China, Chile, Uruguay, and Russia. U.S. researchers are stationed at the South Pole and at several other locations on the continent.

The sparse kitchen trailer for Russia's Bellingshausen Antarctic Station served as home base for our trip. It's named for the Russian explorer Fabian Gottlieb von Bellingshausen, who led expeditions to the Antarctic in the 1820s and who is one of the parties debated to have discovered its existence. We stored baggage and kept warm in the trailer, and the cook made us hot soup. This diplomatic arrangement varies by trip, depending on the race director's negotiation with local officials. It usually involves gifts of fresh fruit and vegetables—precious commodities after 6 months of 24-hour pitch-black winters and infrequent shipments of staples.

Course adjustments occur every year depending on weather and surface conditions. Even the location on King George Island can change since it's subject to written permission from local research stations and science foundations. The race usually requires a wind-chilled climb up Collins Glacier, which is streaked with serrated ice and a thin layer of snow. Runners have slipped and fallen, twisting ankles and breaking ribs. One even hit his head hard enough to result in a concussion. If you have trepidations about running on ice, it's worth considering stabilizers. They are membranes that fit over the soles of your sneakers, dotted with metal studs for increased traction.

Elsewhere on the course, glacial runoff creates small streams. If water is running deep enough to douse ankles, it's bridged with wood planks. Feet plunged in icy cold water will stay in your sneakers the rest of the race. Not only is it uncomfortable, but extremities exposed to freezing temperatures are vulnerable to frostbite and hypothermia, a drop in body temperature that endangers metabolism and bodily functions. Warm, dry feet and hands are essential in cold-weather marathons. You may also discover a few new body parts, such as earlobes, that you wish to keep warm and never worried about in previous races.

Mud is the biggest course hazard because daytime temperatures average just above freezing during the Antarctic summer. Dirt roads connecting the research stations absorb water from melting snow and ice. The mixture swallows your sneakers, as the female front-runner found out the year I ran. Her foot came right out of her sneaker and plunged straight into the mud.

Don't run this race if you need cheering crowds to finish. Antarctica is sparsely populated with government-approved researchers and support personnel. The only on-lookers I saw were three parka-clad Chileans, singing and clenching a bottle of vodka, who offered me a cigarette.

Environmental concerns prevent dispensing water in the disposable bottles or paper cups traditionally found at races. Rehydrating requires three of your own personally labeled bottles, dropped by the race organizer along a 6.5-mile, out-and-back route repeatedly run. When 150 containers from fellow competitors are all packed together in cardboard boxes, only the tops are visible. Quickly locating your bottle is surprisingly difficult unless it's an unusual color or you tie the neck with a distinctive ribbon.

Don't worry about competitors crowding you. The small field quickly spreads out according to ability. Do worry about skuas, fiercely predatory birds with a four-foot wing span that have earned the nickname "Raptors of the South." Skuas raid penguin rooks for eggs and chicks. The scavengers have been known to continue their hunt for food by diving at runners in colorful gear eating energy bars.

Race-day weather was a mild 38 degrees Fahrenheit, but down here there's no telling when a severe temperature drop or storm can set in. Trail-running shoes made of Gortex® or other water-resistant, insulating fabric protect feet better than traditional running shoes. Their thick soles help cushion the mud, but they also add additional weight to your feet. Some people have found regular running shoes adequate, but racing flats aren't a good idea.

Whatever sneakers you select, bring two pairs to the race site given the unpredictable conditions. You'll repeatedly run by the Bellingshausen home base, a convenient route if you're in need of a change of footwear. Warm, waterproof, cold weather gear is necessary pre- and postrace. There's a lot of downtime on the island and you can't return to your ship on command when you finish the race.

An international field with fascinating race résumés is drawn to the bottom of the world. Few elite runners participate because no prize money is awarded. The majority of the pack average four hours to complete the course. My year, the last to come in was a walking quadriplegic. Aided by a cane, he crossed the finish line in under seven hours, despite a sprained ankle caused by a fall on the glacier. Currently, the marathon cutoff time is 6½ hours, and you're required to pass the halfway point in 3 hours and 10 minutes.

The 2-week trip and race registration is an inclusive package deal run by Marathon Tours & Travel. There aren't many alternative races in Antarctica since transportation and events involving this protected territory require challenging logistics and special permission from authorities. Presently, the continent is governed by the Antarctic Treaty, opened for signature in 1959 and currently ratified by 46 nations.

Coming solo on this trip is an excellent idea because the expedition is primarily aboard ship. There's plenty of company at meals, lectures, and on deck, if you feel like socializing. But don't count on getting single-occupancy accommodations. There's a strong likelihood the race will sell out even years in advance, and you'll be assigned a roommate in a shared cabin. It's a great trip for traveling companions who don't run because most of the ten days aboard is spent exploring Antarctica, an experience you're unlikely to repeat in a lifetime.

Meeting a lot of interesting people is inevitable. Who else would venture to the bottom of the world? The year I ran, the captain performed a marriage on the bridge of the ship. The bride in her white dress and the groom in his tux presided over dinner prepared by the chef. Everyone on board was considered a member of the wedding party and drank champagne that the happy couple provided.

An industrious crew ran side-businesses in addition to their day jobs, offering extra services to passengers. In addition to massages, handmade crafts from Russia, nautical

maps, and various other souvenirs were available for pur-
chase, but there was no last-minute running gear to buy.
Load up on energy gels, electrolyte-replacement fluids, and
other essentials before you leave home. If you want to preserve your memories and record results with cameras and
running watches, be sure to pack extra batteries, film, or
disks.

The postrace tour cruising scenic Antarctic inlets reveals
miles of winding, frost-blue glaciers flowing toward shore.
From the deck you can hear the ice snap, crackle, and pop.
Occasionally, huge sections break apart and crumble into
the water. In numerous bays, turquoise-colored icebergs
the size of small buildings grace the water, floating
toward the ocean like sailboats embarking on a distant
voyage.

Day trips by Zodiac boat to heavily populated penguin
rooks make you feel like you're part of the *March of the
Penguins* documentary. Pecking at our thick rubber boots
provided by the ship, the waddling birds proved curious
and willing to overcome any fear of humans. However, their
cuteness is trumped by the unbearable stench from their
excrement, often forcing you to cover your nose.

Swimming in Antarctica is another crowd-pleaser. Deception Bay contains thermal bathwaters, heated by steam
vents on the ocean floor, creating scalding hot spots in otherwise freezing water. We stripped off our cold-weather gear
in frigid outdoor temperatures to reveal bathing suits, and
took a dip in the ocean.

More drastic swims took place after the race. Believe it
or not, several runners celebrated by jumping into the

frigid, 34-degree-Fahrenheit ocean. I wouldn't recommend taking the plunge—a doctor advised me that people have had heart attacks from exposure to such extreme water temperatures.

Antarctica hides its dangerous side well. On race day, rough waters kept one of two ships on the trip from disembarking passengers. The race director was caught between a rock and a hard place. Waiting for half of the marathon runners endangered everyone given the conditions—subfreezing temperatures on a course with no lights, paved roads, or sophisticated emergency medical services, isolated at the bottom of the world.

A spur-of-the-moment decision was made to start the race without half of the runners. Left behind, this group included a team of disabled athletes, who, as we had, just spent thousands of dollars and negotiated two weeks off work for this likely once-in-a-lifetime experience. Stranded on deck, on their boat, they watched us cross the starting line. Fortunately, sometime later they were able to shuttle to the island for a second heat.

Several years later, runners weren't so lucky. That year, no one could safely disembark and the marathon was held on the ship. Circling the deck 344 or 422 times (depending upon which deck you were assigned) and navigating doorways with 6-inch-high foot jambs became the challenge. Whether you can claim the marathon was officially run on the continent, and not at sea, is anybody's guess, but you have to admire such determination.

The trip takes place in February/March, the Southern Hemisphere's summer. Eighteen hours of daylight can keep you up late at night on deck, or socializing at the ship's lounge.

Side trips in South America can be arranged by the tour company. Exploring Patagonia, extra days in Buenos Aires, and other excursions are well worth it, especially since you've taken the time to fly this far south. The 10-day-long cruise of the Antarctic coastline is included in your trip.

BORROWDALE FELL RACE
Climb Me a Mountain

LOCATION: ROSTHWAITE, ENGLAND
MONTH: AUGUST
DISTANCE/AVERAGE FIELD: 17 MILES/500

E-MAIL: len@borrowdalefellrunners.co.uk
WEBSITE: www.borrowdalefellrunners.co.uk

Fell running, originally an English sport, derives its name from the mountains and hills, or fells, gracing northern Britain, especially in the Lake District. There, you'll find some of the world's most beautiful scenery. Endless landscapes of soft green grass blanket the ground, rising in a series of ascents as far as the eye can see. Crests gently slope into valleys, contoured around lakes perfectly nestled in between mountains. The sight gives new meaning to the phrase "God's Country."

The beauty woven into the Borrowdale Fell Race is

deceiving. Conquering six summits on the course, a feat known as peak bagging, demands a climb totaling 6,500 feet. It requires endurance, stamina, and navigational skills.

Fell races are rated for ascent and distance. Borrowdale Fell Race proudly owns the most difficult grade, a Category A. This class requires at least 250 feet of ascent per mile and not more than 20 percent of the race on a road. Distance categories are divided into long, medium, and short courses. Borrowdale's 17-mile length easily exceeds the long category's 12-mile minimum.

Special trainers, or footwear, designed for fell racing effectively grip grass and loose stones on steep terrain while forcing out water and dirt. Runners consider them essential equipment for the multiple crossings over wet ground and calf-deep streams. Rain also proves an obstacle. Weather in the Lake District is notoriously unpredictable and it's not unusual for runners to find themselves caught in cloud cover with limited visibility. One's sense of direction is easily obscured, making it impossible to follow the front-runner and easy to miss dangerous drop-offs.

Numbers for the geographic location of seven race checkpoints are derived from the British National Grid Reference system, a numerical tool similar to longitude and latitude coordinates. Runners are required to be proficient in this navigational skill, and must carry a compass, course map, waterproof tops and bottoms, a whistle, and emergency food.

A paddock across the street from the Scafell Hotel serves as the starting line for this grueling race. Of the six summits along the 17-mile route, the highest is Scafell Pike at 3,209 feet. Course terrain ranges from farm fields and quarries to slate mines and unforgiving climbs with narrow passages known as some of the roughest in England.

Slippery rocks lie in wait on the highest climb, and loose rock, or scree, takes its toll on tired legs. Between holes in the ground, mud, and wet grass, runners easily lose their footing. Even the most seasoned competitors may land headfirst in a bog. Weather conditions can turn so adverse that mountain rescue teams monitor the course, advising competitors along the route of dangerous conditions. Updates on rain, wind, and fog from the BBC Weather report have a prominent spot on the race website, as does a live webcam of the area.

Borrowdale Fell Running Club sponsors the race. Pictures of magnificent scenery, competitors bloodied from taking a spill, a fell running-shoe survey, and a race field groping through fog can be viewed on its website. There are also links to the Scafell Hotel, which sponsors the race, and to additional accommodations, including a bed-and-breakfast in an eighteenth-century farmhouse.

Only experienced fell runners can get a number to compete in what Brits call a "cracking good race." First to apply are accepted when registration opens in the late spring for the August race. There are limited hotel accommodations, but camping out in nearby fields is popular and much less expensive. British tradition is adhered to after runners cross the finish, when tea and sarnis, or sandwiches, are served. A steel band and lots of dancing at the postrace party is in store for exhausted finishers who catch a second wind.

LANTAU MOUNTAIN MARATHON
King of the Hills

LOCATION: LANTAU ISLAND, HONG KONG

MONTH: JANUARY

DISTANCE/AVERAGE FIELD: 18.5 MILES/75, 8.7 MILES/200

TELEPHONE: (Hong Kong) +852-2812-0741

WEBSITE: www.seyonasia.com/Koth/lt

Hong Kong includes a handful of islands that dot the South China Sea. Lantau is the largest, marked by steep mountains swiftly rising from the water, outlining the island. It's home to Tian Tan, or Big Buddha, a 10-story-high figure made of bronze that glistens in the sunlight. Sitting in the lotus position halfway up a 3,064-foot mountain on the course, the "Enlightened One" watches over you from a distance. The closer you get, the more you appreciate his grandeur, a much-needed inspiration during the race.

Despite its 18.5-mile distance, nearly 8 miles short of a traditional marathon, Lantau Mountain Marathon considers itself well titled when measured by the Naismith Rule. The formula, popular in Great Britain with fell mountain runners, calculates the time it takes to climb an uphill course versus a flat road distance. Entered into a GPS program, compared to a flat course, this marathon measures 50K (31 miles) and the half-marathon 23K (14.3 miles). That's 60 percent "additional mileage" for each race.

Lantau Mountain Marathon is part of the three-race series in Hong Kong known as King of the Hills, which

"BECAUSE IT'S THERE"

includes the Sai Kung Marathon and the Taipo Marathon. Enter it and you might find the event more of a climb than a run. But, standing on top of mountain ridges so enormous that they dare you to climb them, you definitely consider yourself crowned.

Race registration takes place on the ferry to Mui Wo from Pier 6 at Central Ferry Pier, the regular commuting boat to and from mainland Hong Kong. The race director balances himself between seats when encountering choppy waters, checking people in and handing them race numbers. If you miss the boat, jump on the next ferry and try to catch up with the group on the island.

Once docked at Mui Wo, we boarded buses at the nearby depot. Waiting on line, some took the opportunity to run into the local store to replenish water supplies. Although there are water stops on the marathon and half-marathon courses, climbs are so rugged, it's prudent to carry multiple water bottles, snacks, and energy drinks.

The race begins at Nam Shan Pavilion, a public park picnic area in a wooded ravine. A small banner hung between two trees marks the start. The race director yells "go," and officially times the race by his running watch. The portion of the race in shaded, cool woods on a downhill hiking trail is short-lived, as you soon start your first climb. Exposed rocks littered all over the trail are difficult to navigate, but can literally offer a "foot up" the mountain.

Runners are quite civil about letting competitors pass and passing competitors. It's a good policy, since the higher you go, the more treacherous the falloff. I had to stop often to catch my breath. The breathtaking views made it worthwhile.

Gazing back at boats crossing the harbor from the South China Sea, framed by the contour of the mountains, I briefly forgot my fatigue.

At the top of Sheung Tung pass, the marathon and half-marathon split. Race officials are there to ensure competitors make the right turns. The mountain ridge course becomes what locals call "shiggyish," or overgrown. A bit of calf-length "shiggy bashing" means bushwhacking is required, with scratches to follow.

From sea level at dockside, you're headed toward Lin Fa Shan at 2,513 feet. The altitude climb means drinking ample water is important. Even on a temperate day, steep climbs and difficult footwork make you very thirsty. A word of caution: The sun is quite potent on these windy mountaintops. Be sure to carry high-SPF sunscreen and reapply.

Farther along the ridges, steep drops on either side of the trails unnerve even the most intrepid runner. Several forks in the course are obscure, leaving you unsure of which way to turn. The small yellow paper signs marked K.O.T.H., King of the Hills, are easily missed. Sometimes runners make a wrong turn and find it impossible to make up the extra mileage.

Down the mountain, steep, narrow dirt paths are more suited to hiking boots than to running sneakers. The lack of switchbacks to lessen downhill gravity leaves nothing to break a fall, making for a tenuous descent. During my race, trepidation set in when small loose rocks caused slippery steps, throwing me off balance and seriously slowing my time. A mountain rescue team member sweeps the course for good reason. In races past, people have fallen or gotten lost in the woods and had to be saved. The good news is that, despite the isolation, cell phones usually work, aiding the rescue.

The first 18K forces runners to climb up and across mountaintops from sea level, then down to the water's edge before the second series of mountain climbs begin. Big Buddha sits mid-range on the second ascent, inspiring prayer whether or not you're a believer. A bell within Buddha, which rings 108 times a day, symbolizes escape for the 108 troubles of mankind. Your trouble today is whether you can finish this race.

Hundreds of tourists crowd souvenir stands and parking lots at the base of the "Enlightened One" in a short section of the course that leaves the trail. Here runners cross a checkpoint and must clock in before heading into a wooded area again. After Big Buddha, the toughest section is in store, a 1,640-foot climb over a mile stretch.

The third checkpoint sits at Pak Kung Au, halfway down the mountain, on the final section of the race. Having conquered ascents totaling thousands of feet, several disappointed runners were stopped at this juncture. Just minutes past the cutoff time, they were told that they could continue but they wouldn't qualify for a finisher's certificate. Medals are not awarded for completing this grueling race.

The finish line is back by the race start. Competitors gather nearby on benches by a cooler of beer, trading stories before catching public transportation back to the docks. The field consists of mostly Hong Kongers and southern Chinese, with an even split between Chinese and expatriates in the half-marathon. The marathon, however, is 80 percent Chinese; they seem to enjoy longer endurance events.

Hong Kong International Airport is on Lantau Island, though it's barely visible from the race course. When your vacation ends and you have to fly home, you'll be back on this island. You'll think of it in a new light, having run the Lantau Mountain Marathon.

MONGOLIA SUNRISE TO SUNSET
Far and Away

LOCATION: HOVSGOL NATIONAL PARK, MONGOLIA
MONTH: JULY
DISTANCE/AVERAGE FIELD: 62.1 MILES/15, 26.4 MILES/50

TELEPHONE: (China) +86-21-6266-0844-896
WEBSITE: www.ultramongolia.com

Relatively untouched by civilization, traveling to Mongolia is like stepping back into another era. Located south of Siberia and north of China, reaching the race start at Lake Hovsgol is an adventure in and of itself. Flying into the country's capital, Buyant-Ukhaa, better known as Ulan Bator, you're still 360 miles from your destination.

A local flight to the lake's nearest airport may be canceled due to the weather-dependent, grass landing strip, which becomes too muddy to handle landing gear when it rains. If you're detoured, the alternate airport's arrival terminal is a wood hut, where you'll crowd into one of two vans for a 6-hour ride over bumpy grassland.

One year, a van broke down. There were no gas stations, road signs, or mobile phone signals for miles around. Thankfully the drivers were able to fiddle underneath the hood and interchange enough parts between the two vehicles to fix the problem. Hours later, runners finally arrived at Camp Toilogt, a clearing south of Lake Hovsgol.

Far from civilization, nomads provide accommodations by setting up Gers, circular tents insulated with cotton and felt covers over wood frames. Inside stands a log-burning fire vented up the middle of the tent. Heat is essential as Arctic winds sweep down past Siberia into Northern Mongolia. July temperatures range from freezing at night to T-shirt weather during the day. Runners sleep three to a Ger while a large tent houses a shower room, kitchen, and eating area. Water is drawn from Lake Hovsgol, one of the largest freshwater reserves in the world.

The race begins before dawn by the campsite, at an altitude of 5,400 feet. It's dark enough to require head lamps at the beginning of your run. At sunrise, you can store your light in day packs, which are stuffed with food and emergency gear that's required to be carried throughout the race. The first part of the course passes damp, moss-covered pine woods, along rough dirt roads following Lake Hovsgol. Then the route heads inland toward Chichee Pass, at 7,550 feet the highest altitude on the course. It's not lack of sleep that causes you to see race officials dressed up like Genghis Khan, in long brocade coats and hats, riding ponies. Bred to run for miles, the swift horse and its intrepid rider can appear out of nowhere, just when a runner thinks that no one is around.

An old mining road takes competitors back down to 5,525 feet, along a trail that sometimes disappears through pine woods, alpine meadows, and dried riverbeds. Then, prepare yourself for the second and steepest climb of the day, a 1,000-plus-foot ascent to Khirvesteg Pass. Thick undergrowth and fallen trees obscure the trail, making trail markers extremely difficult to locate. The heat is so intense that the 650-foot descent into the valley, to the next water station, seems too long. The course continues along the lakeshore, where marathoners finish at Camp Toilogt.

At this point, ultramarathoners have yet to complete a 36-mile lower loop that includes a 6,500-foot ascent at Jankhai Pass. Arriving at camp, it's not unusual for these ambitious runners to rethink their choice and downgrade to the marathon. More courageous souls continue the race, although average finishing times increase by 50 percent. Even shortly after the race start, one ultramarathoner decided to walk the challenging 62.1-mile course, finishing in 19 hours.

Shamanism lingers as a religion and pays homage to environmental concerns. The race coordinators caution runners to avoid littering lest they upset the spirits. This eco-friendly race dispenses plastic bags to participants, and requests that they pick up bottles and bags during the race. Garbage can be dropped off at one of the three aid stations on each loop of the course.

Runners are encouraged to follow local customs, like

rotating three times around ovoos, small rock piles that serve as navigational aids. Locals use them to worship the mountains and sky. Runners follow these unorthodox suggestions to avoid bad luck during their race.

Thin ribbons tied to trees or small wooden arrows stuck in ovoos can prove too subtle as course markers. Wooded areas and animal tracks from reindeer and other wildlife can also obscure the route. Confusion sets in at several points. Looking for the front-runners is fruitless with no more than fifty competitors involved. It can be a bit worrisome, and runners have gotten lost before race officials have ridden to the rescue.

Long-haired yaks graze on the race course, along with camels, wild sheep, ibex (wild mountain goats), bears, moose, and 200 species of birds. The sight of cattle may seem fairly benign, but some reportedly have chased runners.

Predawn morning weather is cold enough to warrant windproofs until temperatures warm up by midday, at which point you'll be taking off layers of clothing to prevent overheating. Bananas, biscuits, and water are offered every 5K, but aid stations aren't necessarily manned, adding to the isolation.

Although runners travel a long way to complete this race, it's called before dusk to ensure everyone's safety. Elevation changes and the rugged, off-road course are so tiring that most people struggle to make it to the finish line.

At the end of the race, there's no wait for the showers as competitors straggle in at different times. Water is heated to just below boiling on a woodstove. Adjusting the heat level takes practice, and a little bit of scalding is hard to avoid. After you dry off, a bountiful barbecue and locally grown organic produce await.

Bringing backup running gear, such as sneakers or trail shoes and race-day clothing, is essential. There's nowhere to buy additional equipment. It's important to remember that weather can take a turn for the worse, so pack accordingly. The same is not true for souvenirs. Buying opportunities appear from the middle of nowhere. Unique items turn up, such as yak hair sweaters warmer than cashmere, and handwoven or animal-skin blankets, hats, and waistcoats.

Torn between Russian and Chinese politics, Mongolia is an underdeveloped country with a sparse population. One-fifth the size of the U.S., it's occupied by only about three million people. Despite being landlocked, the country boasts a one-boat navy that patrols Lake Hovsgol. The ship was transported there section by section.

Visiting runners are warmly welcomed and lavishly entertained by performances of Buyant-Ukhaa's Cirque du Soleil–like troupe of amazing acrobats and contortionists. Despite its remote location, the entire trip including travel to Mongolia lasts only 8 days, departing from Beijing. You can add on extra time by the lake for horseback riding, kayaking, and fishing.

The July race date is close to Mongolia's National Holiday, July 11th to July 13th, when the Naadam Festival is held. Roughly translated, it means "three manly games" and consists of competitions in Mongolian wrestling, horse racing, and archery. The celebrations commence with elaborate ceremonies in the capital city of Ulan Bator, as well as in smaller towns across the country. It's worth extending your trip to witness the competition, which has been in existence for centuries. If you're looking to get far away from it all, and you're unfazed by a lack of creature comforts, this is a race worth your serious consideration.

MOUNT KILIMANJARO MARATHON® & SUMMIT CLIMB
Barefoot Runners

LOCATION: MOSHI, TANZANIA

MONTH: JUNE

DISTANCE/AVERAGE FIELD: 26.2 MILES/100, 13.1 MILES/10, 6.2 MILES/30

TELEPHONE: 702-279-0646

WEBSITE: www.mtkilimanjaromarathon.com

The Mount Kilimanjaro Marathon, Half-Marathon, and 10K (6.2 miles) start at the foot of Africa's tallest mountain. The majestic, snowcapped mountain is the backdrop for local life in the small town of Moshi. Children chase you down the street in bare feet to high-five you. Women in colorful turbans selling fruit call out to passersby, hoping to make a sale. There's a romance to running in Africa, reminiscent of the great novels and movies set there.

The 10.5K four-loop course for the marathon starts in front of your hotel with curious locals gathered out front. The half-marathon and 10K follow the same route, a paved road that turns to dirt as runners head out of town. Small two-room homes and an occasional farm dot the course. A crowing rooster or mooing cow can be heard from animal pens, fenced in with odd bits of wire. Their pungent scent fills the air on a 90-degree-Fahrenheit day.

At the edge of town sits a small white chapel. The year I ran, a choir sang inside. A cappella music floated out the open-air windows along the course. The harmony was so compelling, one competitor actually stopped mid-race to enter the church, sit in a pew, and listen.

A forest at the end of the road marks the turnaround, leading you back into town. There, a large market is crowded with stands filled with colorful fruits and vegetables, and stalls packed with trinkets. Shoppers and merchants stopped their transactions to cheer us on.

Unfortunately, the town bus depot is located on the course. Thick, jet-black exhaust spews from colorfully decorated vehicles, obscuring their bright, hand-painted designs. With each repetition of this four-loop course I dreaded bus drivers starting their engines and pulling into the street, knowing my toxic intake would be intensified. Despite being desperate for oxygen, I held my breath to avoid inhaling the foul emissions.

Children along the course sometimes ran miles alongside competitors, "adopting" them during the race. Running is a way of life in Africa. People struggle to afford food and shelter, let alone cars. Instead of a school bus, children use their feet to get back and forth to school. Locals jog to the market and to visit neighbors on the other side of town.

In economically developing countries, running is an accessible sport. It doesn't require expensive equipment or a special facility to train. Africa, and particularly Kenya, is home to many of the world's greatest long-distance runners, such as Catherine Ndereba and Paul Tergat. A Swedish physiologist at Denmark's Copenhagen Muscle Research Centre studied Kenyans in an attempt to discover their competitive advantage. He concluded that they can resist fatigue longer. He credits their thinner calves with taking less energy to move, and muscles that genetically produce less lactate enzyme, allowing them to squeeze more mileage from oxygen intake.

You more clearly understand the favorable genetics when you're struggling in sweltering heat and locals in bare feet whiz past you like race cars. Africans who were better off ran in too small Keds—thin white soles with no tread. The top of the canvas was cut out, allowing their toes to stick out over the edge. It's humbling to tourists in shorts and singlets made of technically correct perspiration-wicking fabric, and well-cushioned sneakers with thick soles.

A water shortage my year forced me off-course to belly up to the local bar for a club soda. Drink in hand, I stood alongside curious regulars at the water hole in my running shorts and singlet. The race director tried to make good on the lack of liquid by driving alongside runners and offering them bottled water. Improvements now include ten water stations on route, colorfully decorated, with manpower provided by local seminaries.

Race numbers were rustic, a torn sheet with my first name in felt-tip marker, enabling English-speaking spectators to personally cheer me on by name. The mostly American field varied greatly in athletic prowess; marathon finishing times ranged from 3 to 6 hours. The heat was tolerable because part of the course was run in the shade. Still, some had difficulty with the 90-degree-Fahrenheit temperatures.

No start or finish clock graced the race. Running watches recorded splits and finish times. Race awards included a medal, certificate, and dried gourd with an African woman carved into the shell. Local artisans created several more unique race mementos. One colorful screen print read "Mount Kilimanjaro Marathon" in a scene of grass plains and table-top trees.

Hearty souls, including myself, continued the challenge after the marathon by climbing the highest mountain in Africa. With 48 hours of rest, we traded in our sneakers for hiking boots, for a 5-day 19,344-feet climbing excursion. Above a layer of clouds, I stood atop Uhuru Peak, the highest point on Mount Kilimanjaro, to conquer one of the seven summits, the tallest mountains on every continent.

Extending the usual 4-day climb schedule by an additional day or two is preferable for properly acclimatizing. Most tours have an average daily altitude ascent of 3,234 feet and almost 4,000 feet to scale the night you summit. Yet, recommended altitude climbs for trekkers range from 1,000 to 1,600 feet a day. Despite the rigorous climb and altitude gain, there is no medical prescreening required.

Although some marathoners chose to climb Mount Kilimanjaro before running the marathon, many of us who waited until afterward were less dehydrated and exhausted during the climb. As if runners needed another challenge, a 50-mile mountain bike race that takes place outside of Moshi is an additional option. Safaris are a popular excursion, a worthwhile add-on if you've never witnessed zebras resting their necks on the backs of their brethren, giraffes munching on table-top trees, and lion cubs playfully rolling in tall grass.

LIKE MOUNT KILIMANJARO?

There's another race run at the foot of Africa's tall-est mountain. Check out the Kilimanjaro Marathon, Half-Marathon, and 5K at www.kilimanjaromarathon.com.

MOUNT WASHINGTON ROAD RACE
Only One Hill
LOCATION: GORHAM, NEW HAMPSHIRE
MONTH: JUNE
DISTANCE/AVERAGE FIELD: 7.6 MILES/1,000

TELEPHONE: 603-863-2537
WEBSITE: www.mountwashingtonroadrace.com

What really signals the start of the Mount Washington Road Race is the race director's tongue-in-cheek reminder that "there's only one hill." Then a cannon fires, and run-ners head straight to the summit, scaling a vertical of 4,650 feet. Undeterred by the climb, hopeful participants clamor to get into the annually sold-out 7.6-mile race. The 1,100 spots are selected by lottery in early March.

The grade on the course averages 11.5 percent, max-ing out at 22 percent on the last 50 yards to the top. This legendary stretch, mercilessly left for the finish, has even elite runners walking. It's named Sheep's Back Hairpin for the turn in the road. "Steep grade" road warning signs for tractor trailers start at 5 percent, so consider yourself challenged. Adding to your running woes is thin air. The altitude at the summit is 6,288 feet.

The unpredictable weather on top of the mountain is intimidating and legendary. U.S. Forest Service signs warn that you're in an area "with the worst weather in America," thanks to being located at the juncture of three major storm tracks. Rain, sleet, or snow can stop you dead in your tracks year-round. Visibility is often less than 100 feet, since clouds envelop the mountain 60 percent of the time. Temperatures dip as low as 20 degrees Fahrenheit, despite a late June race date. Clouds sweep across the mountain as swiftly as smoke escapes from a chimney when winds kick up as high as 60 miles per hour. It's still only a fraction of the 231-miles-per-hour wind that tore across Mount Washington in 1934, the fastest speed recorded on Earth.

Weather conditions cut the course short in 2002. Understandably, the race director reserves the right to cancel the competition for any reason. Visitors have died from exposure even in the middle of the summer. Severe weather is why L.L. Bean selected Mount Washington to field-test its outerwear. You'll need to rely on your own kit. Participants are asked to send warm clothing to the top, including mittens, hats, and winter jackets. It's a good idea since temperatures normally drop 3 to 5 degrees for every vertical 1,000 feet. Mylar heat sheets are provided by the organizers at the finish line. It's usually so cold up top that organizers collect electronic timing chips back down at the bottom.

As if all this isn't difficult enough to contend with, the mileposts along the course can be confusing. Since the race is held on an auto road that technically starts a tenth of a mile back, mile 1 is actually only .9 miles into the race. It's a discrepancy that continues at each mile signpost for the duration of the race. Three water stops are on the course, one stationed at the summit. There'd be more, but it's difficult to transport liquids and establish aid stations on a mountain with unpredictable weather.

A 3:02:00 cutoff time is strictly enforced. The clock is stopped and any remaining runners are asked to accept a ride down. The course record is 56:41, but you can predict your own time with a calculator available on the website, based on your average race time.

The Sherman Adams Summit House provides shelter to cog railway passengers, hikers, and a limited number of runners after the race. Its views of the Presidential Mountain range are spectacular, but it can only accommodate—and warm up with hot chocolate—a quarter of the race finishers. Exhausted competitors are carpooled down after the race. The tear-off tab on race bibs allows cars to drive up to the summit prerace, if the driver collects two stubs.

The idea for this weather-challenged event was conceived in 1904, when George Foster, a medical school student, impressed his friends by climbing to the top in 1 hour and 42 minutes, faster than a car could make the trip. To ensure his legacy—albeit 32 years later—friends organized a road race in his honor. It was held on and off until 1966, and is now an annual event. Its reputation has spread, drawing international runners including the women's six-time champion from as far away as the Czech Republic.

PIKES PEAK MARATHON® & PIKES PEAK ASCENT®
Uphill Climb

LOCATION: MANITOU SPRINGS, COLORADO

MONTH: AUGUST

DISTANCE/AVERAGE FIELD: 26.2 MILES/800, 13.3 MILES/2,000

TELEPHONE: 719-473-2625

WEBSITE: www.pikespeakmarathon.org

Stunning vistas at the top of Pikes Peak inspired the lyrics for "America the Beautiful." Keep that in mind while you're running to the summit in the Pikes Peak Marathon or Pikes Peak Ascent, the half-marathon held the day before the 26.2-mile race. Don't be intimidated by the fact that General Zebulon Pike, an explorer for whom the mountain was named, failed to make it up the 14,115-foot ascent in 1806. His party was turned back by heavy snows in mid-November, but this race takes place in more temperate August weather.

Qualifying times from the last five years are required for both the marathon and the half-marathon. Additional criteria are considered for entry, such as finishing times at previous Pikes Peak races. Despite filtering out the inexperienced, the marathon sells out in under an hour and the ascent fills up within months, when registration opens in March. Runners are divided into two waves, a half hour apart, for the ascent and two fields with the same starting time for the marathon.

Manitou Springs, a charming town reminiscent of Wild West outposts, now filled with coffee shops and art galleries, hosts the starting line in front of City Hall. Runners are requested to respect the local residents. Reminders include signs in front yards politely warning those looking for a restroom not to "water the lawn" or else risk being arrested for indecent exposure. There are "use them, lose them" rules for headphones, so don't plan on having music take your mind off things, unless you are playing it inside your head.

Despite a paved road at the beginning of the course, the first couple of miles are still no bargain. The incline just to reach Barr Trail in Pike National Forest is the worst average grade of the race. At 13.4 percent, the ascent forces many runners to slow down considerably shortly after crossing the starting line. The often-heard advice "Don't start out fast; you'll burn out early" counts twice here.

On this uphill slant sits the infamous Cog Railway Depot. Departing trains painstakingly take over three hours to climb Pikes Peak and return. In 1889, Simmons Beautyrest Mattress Company founder Zalmon Simmons built the cog railway, then the world's highest, deciding his climb on a mule was much too exhausting.

Unlike Simmons, competitors must run up the mountain. Entering Barr Trail, you're immediately scaling a narrow switchback, steep enough to warrant a wooden guardrail. It forces competitors into a single-file line, but the field has already spread out, so the bottlenecks aren't too bad. If you want to pass, competitors are happy to oblige. Protruding rocks spring up throughout the trail; tripping over one emphasizes the importance of lifting up your feet.

Past mile 4, every once in a while the trail flattens or treats you to a short downhill, so you can pick up your pace. It's all relative, because the first 10 miles of the race rises 6,000 vertical feet. You're now running at an elevation of 11,950 feet, with one-third less oxygen than at sea level. One runner described fellow competitors at this point as having "turned into walking zombies."

Such a severe climb increases the importance of drinking a lot of water, offered at frequent aid stations, located every 1 to 3 miles. U.S. Forest Service permits require that all litter must be carried out. Runners must hang on to empty cups, gel foils, and energy food wrappers until they reach the next aid station.

Hydrating 2,800 runners over two days, at water stations on a high-altitude trail race, is a challenge. Volunteers are required to camp out on the mountain for the weekend. They either hand-pump water through a filter system or pipe it through several thousand feet of temporary hose laid by an operations team. Aid-station volunteers equipped with windproofs, backpacks, and poles resemble weekend hikers more than traditional race personnel.

Weather is unpredictable above the 12,000-foot tree line, where temperatures can vary as much as 50 degrees Fahrenheit from the morning lows at the race start. At this altitude, lightning bolts are too close for comfort. In the 2005 Pikes Peak Ascent, a woman survived a strike, though the rubber tips on her sneakers melted and burned. In the past, officials have turned back runners at the A-Frame checkpoint, at 11,950 feet, due to inclement weather higher up.

Sweat Check is a service provided for half-marathoners on Pikes Peak Ascent, affording you a change into dry, warm clothes at the finish. Gear is bagged, numbered, and transported to the summit on the day of their race. It's suggested that you pack a long-sleeve shirt, sweatpants, windbreaker, socks, warm hat, and gloves. For marathoners, a change of clothes at the turnaround point on the mountaintop is also allowed. Unlike half-marathoners who are competing the day before, you're running back down the mountain, so there's no shuttle to take your clothes up. You'll need a buddy willing to meet you on top of Pikes Peak with your gear.

The final 2,165-foot push to the summit has an unforgiving grade averaging over 12 percent. The most difficult section is dubbed "16 Golden Stairs," named for the final 32 switchbacks to the top. As the trail winds its way around giant boulders, frequent step-ups over a foot in height give you an idea why the marathon's moniker is "America's Ultimate Challenge." Literally above-the-cloud views are potent enough to get you past signs signaling that there's still 1 mile to the summit.

Finally, a banner and checkpoint marks the top of the ascent. Thankful half-marathon finishers are shuttled back down the mountain on their Saturday race day. On Sunday, marathoners are only halfway through. This turnaround point, exposed to temperature drops, winds, and quixotic weather, makes runners anxious to start down.

The descent can be just as challenging. The downhill climb requires braking by tired legs. Runners have worn bike helmets to protect their head in case they fall on the rocks. After the long reverse route down, leaving the rocks, stones, and bumpy path on Barr Trail for the paved streets in Manitou Springs provides a little more steady footing.

Cutoff times for each race and wave start are enforced at two trail checkpoints, as well as at the finish line. They are strictly observed, and even shortened if severe weather occurs. Marathoners must officially finish in 10 hours—a very long day, even for spectators. If you're not a front-runner, don't expect cheering crowds at the end of the race.

Hot springs nearby provide relief for aching, tired muscles, with many competitors staying at local hotels. But not before they pack the small-town streets of Manitou Springs to celebrate their achievement. The cozy postrace atmosphere in town enhances the special sense of camaraderie in this unique, challenging event.

LIKE SCALING PEAKS?

If mountain peaks are your passion, try running the European alps. The Jungfrau Marathon, MiniMarathon (2.6 miles), and Mile, in Interlaken, Switzerland, is held in September: www.jungfrau-marathon.ch.

There's another mountain to climb at the Marathon du Mont-Blanc (26.2 miles), Cross du Mont-Blanc (14.3 miles), and 10K (6.2 miles), traversing the Chamonix region of the French Alps: www.montblancmarathon.net.

SIBERIAN ICE MARATHON
Coldest Race on Record

LOCATION: OMSK, RUSSIA

MONTH: JANUARY

DISTANCE/AVERAGE FIELD: 13 MILES/400, 4.3 MILES/500

TELEPHONE: (Russia) +7-3812-242-567

WEBSITE: www.runsim.ru/ice/about

At 13 miles, the Siberian Ice Marathon may have kept its 26.2-mile name because seriously frigid temperatures make it feel like you're running twice the distance. Organizers claim to have held the coldest race in history, in 2001, when the thermometer bottomed out at minus 44 degrees Fahrenheit. That year, although 223 runners registered, only 134 showed up for the deep freeze at the starting line. Most of those competitors slowed to a glacial halt in the physically immobilizing weather, leaving only 11 comrades to cross the finish line.

Successive races have recorded higher temperatures, including a balmy 10-degree-Fahrenheit day in 2003. This may be one reason the field has increased to almost 1,000 runners for both races. The majority of competitors are locals accustomed to the cold—so much so that dressing in costume or shorts is not unheard of. Another reason may be their desire to receive the "special warm sports cap" included in the latest race-participant package.

In frigid January weather, the 21K (13 mile) race is a six-loop course. It makes a lot of sense. Aid stations can be repeatedly used at fewer locations, and there's less time for poured water to freeze. Race organizers must be greatly relieved to recruit fewer volunteers to man them.

A short loop also allows most of the course to be conveniently close to town resources, such as medical services to treat injuries like frostbite. Spectators or loved ones (and that's a lot of love) who accompanied you to this toe-numbing scene will also be thankful for easier access to the heated buildings.

The race begins in Central Square and continues along the banks of the frozen Irtysh River. It passes an architecturally interesting historic district (you'll need the distraction). Surprisingly, the temperature doesn't severely slow down the elite runners. The course record is 1:10:00 for men, and 1:23:00 for women. The 7K (4.3 mile) race loops twice around, allowing much faster relief from frozen conditions than its 21K compatriot.

Hot tea is served to runners, although at these temperatures tea, sweat, and the tears you'll be crying can freeze fairly fast. Every drop of moisture solidifies quickly. Exposed hair peeking out from under your skullcap or the beard on your face becomes iced. The white-tinged strands artificially age you. Frozen eyelashes clamp lids shut, leaving competitors to see through a squint. Even the slightest amount of condensation solidifies, including the breath you exhale during the race. Neck gaiters, keeping your chin and nose warm, cause enough moisture to build ice formations around your face.

Siberia's frosty weather and isolation is legendary. The

city of Omsk, called "the gateway to Siberia," is a 2-day train ride from Moscow. Known throughout Russian history as a cold, desolate place, it's been the perfect spot to exile political prisoners and other undesirables.

Fyodor Dostoyevsky was sentenced to eight years in prison here after being arrested as a political activist. It was considered a fate worse than death. Indeed, Tsar Nikolai I sent Dostoyevsky to Omsk instead of carrying out his death sentence, but not before tormenting him by purposely taking him through the stages leading up to execution. A two-story-high bronze statue of the writer, portrayed in an abyss of moral and psychological despair, hovers over the third kilometer of the multi-loop course, so you'll repeatedly pass it. Omsk State Dostoyevsky Literary Museum is also en route, housing a re-creation of the tortured writer's prison cell, including his foot shackles. His fate is a convenient reminder during your race that things could be worse than your freezing feet.

Dangers in this extreme adventure race include frostbite, especially on extremities, and cold-induced asthma. These serious risks intensify the need to train in subfreezing temperatures ahead of time, to say the least. A precise amount of thermal underwear layers and the right type of jacket are essential. Overheating produces sweat that easily freezes and lowers your body temperature. Many runners wear masks or at least some protection to cover their face, while carefully planning for unobstructed, moisture-laden, heavy breaths to escape into the air.

Still up for the trip? Submit your application online or

by mail. After entry forms are reviewed, registration is by invitation, enabling you to get the necessary visa to visit the area.

Ice-carved cathedrals and other elaborate sculptures decorate the city as Siberians celebrate Christmas, on January 7, in the Russian Orthodox tradition. Saint Nicholas costumes with white fur-trimmed, red ankle-length coats are worn by runners or volunteers at aid stations.

Immediately after the race, finishers are taken into a forest for a huge Christmas buffet of traditional foods, champagne, and vodka. Russian baths are also featured—first, a steam to take the chill off, then your body is whipped with a birch twig to stimulate circulation. Afterward you roll around in a snowdrift. Repeat three times and the first one to dinner is the winner.

One competitor quipped after nearly a week that it was easy to see how Napoleon and Hitler were defeated when they tried to invade this territory. If Tsar Nikolai I had had the chance, he might have ordered Dostoyevsky to run the Ice Marathon, to add to the long list of punishments the banished writer suffered.

EAT, DRINK, AND BE MERRY

Some races are just plain fun and that's all that you want them to be. Find the right event and it may not be so much about when you cross the finish line, but how you enjoyed your time on the road.

When a competitor dressed like Cleopatra is literally being carried on a throne by runners costumed as slaves, so what if you slow down to watch the spectacle on the race course? Or, perhaps you're running at one of the world's most famous racetracks and want to soak in the scenery.

Races in this section may convince you to stop and smell the roses, eat fresh-shucked oysters, or taste wine during a race. Believe it or not, there are competitions that celebrate the best things in life, rather than pressure you to set a personal best.

Of course, if you feel uncomfortable with the idea of taking it easy during a race, you can always run your heart out and enjoy yourself afterward. It's your choice, but the unique aspect of these races may put a new spin on how or when you want to cross the finish line.

KENTUCKY DERBY FESTIVAL MARATHON & MINIMARATHON
A Day at the Races

LOCATION: LOUISVILLE, KENTUCKY

MONTH: APRIL

DISTANCE/AVERAGE FIELD: 26.2 MILES/2,000, 13.1 MILES/10,000

TELEPHONE: 502-584-6383

WEBSITE: www.derbyfestivalmarathon.com

Southern hospitality and horse-racing are hallmarks of the Kentucky Derby. Now they're shared by the Kentucky Derby Marathon and miniMarathon, held on the last Saturday in April, a week before the Derby. The starting line in Iroquois Park is set on a picturesque 739-acre expanse covered with the state's famous bluegrass; it's so named because when grown to its natural 2-to-3-foot height, a blue flower blooms.

Runners at the celebration-filled start watch 50 colorful hot-air balloons decorate the sky in a hot-air balloon race orchestrated with the starting gun. Competitors circle the exterior of the park designed by Frederick Law Olmsted, the same architect who designed New York City's Central Park.

Runners juiced as Thoroughbred horses rounding a turn at Churchill Downs race toward the famous track, its often-photographed twin spires in sight. Originally built in 1875, the complex has undergone a recent $121 million renovation, and now shares space with all kinds of events, including Rolling Stones concerts and marathons.

Runners enter the track through an underground passage leading to the infield at the far turn. Rounding the inside track, they pass the starting line that millions of people will be watching on TV one week later, when the gates are filled with hopeful, anxious fillies and colts competing for the first jewel in the Triple Crown of Thoroughbred Racing. One mile is run on the interior blacktop before exiting through a tunnel underneath the historic spires. Barbaro, the 2006 Derby champion later injured at the Preakness, now has his ashes interred by an entrance gate near the race course.

If you'd like to check out the Derby day competition or feel your oats by running near horses, the course winds its way through the paddocks. Here the most elite three-year-old thoroughbreds will be mounted by jockeys before the horse race of a lifetime.

Horses prepping for the Derby are out on the track being trained for their big day. Blinders ensure they're not distracted by thousands of runners streaming through the complex. Live on the big screen, runners are photographed racing through Churchill Downs, while the sound system replays announcers calling previous Kentucky Derby horse races.

Leaving the track, the route follows 4th Street into downtown Louisville where the marathon and miniMarathon part ways. Longer-distance runners head to Cherokee Park, another

Olmsted landmark. MiniMarathoners cross the finish line on Market Street and 6th Street. Marathoners are greeted by a loud and supportive crowd at River Road, along the waterfront. Thousands of revelers who've been celebrating at a daylong Derby Party cheer everyone on.

The miniMarathon, over 35 years old, is the more senior of the two races. A field of 10,000 people sells out a month before the race. The 7-year-old marathon has a much smaller number of competitors—close to 2,000—but the race director doesn't limit the split between the two distances. So, the first 12,000 competitors to apply get a number, no matter which race they ultimately choose.

Most participants come from close by, with 65 percent calling either Kentucky or Indiana home, while another 35 percent travel from the East Coast. This popular race has more than doubled in size over the last several years. A cutoff time of 6 hours applies to both the marathon and the miniMarathon.

The race takes place during the Derby Festival, a two-week-long celebration before the world-renowned horse race. Marathon and miniMarathon weekend includes one of the largest firework displays in North America. Thirty minutes in length, magnificent bursts of color are set to music. Festival tents include much wine and beer, not to mention Kentucky bourbon drinks, plus regional and national bands. Southern barbecue ensures that you'll never be hungry. The menu features chicken, ribs, and pulled pork. An illuminated hot-air balloon show takes place the night before the race. The billowing balloons floating across the sky are choreographed to music.

MARATHON DU MÉDOC
The Longest Marathon in the World—
For a Good Reason

LOCATION: PAUILLAC, FRANCE

MONTH: SEPTEMBER

DISTANCE/AVERAGE FIELD: 26.2 MILES/8,500

TELEPHONE: (France) +33-556-59-17-20

WEBSITE: www.marathondumedoc.com

Le Marathon le Plus Long du Monde," is the Marathon du Médoc slogan. It's not called "the longest marathon in the world" because it exceeds the standard 26.2 mile race, but because wine is served to runners along a course winding through the most famous vineyards in France, which extends even the most dedicated runner's finish.

Fifty-nine châteaux in the world-renowned Médoc wine region open their vineyards to runners and host wine-tasting tables. Respectful of their precious ruby red commodity, celebrated since the 1800s, most tastings are served in glasses instead of plastic cups. Racing becomes secondary for many, especially at Château Lafite-Rothschild, a premiere cru, the province's highest wine classification. When I participated, runners stood politely in line at this tasting, a more crowded table than most, until they received their well-deserved glass. There was no pushing or shoving—in fact competitors in front passed the spoils to the back of the pack, as you would with friends at a dinner party.

But what's a good wine without good food to accompany

it? Race food has a French flair—runners indulged in biscuits, charcuterie, and croissants not only at rest stops but also from generous handouts by bakers, butchers, and spectators. Even chocolate could be found on the course. Of course, water was served along with the wine, paired with fruit slices, to provide more traditional race fare.

A fresh-shucked oyster bar awaits you at mile 23, complete with 22,000 opened shells resting on an ice bed. Accompaniments include fresh lemon, cocktail sauce, and—despite Bordeaux's famous red wine reputation—white wine for those who prefer it with fish. The oyster bar alone kept me inspired for 10 miles. A little farther up the road fresh-grilled filet mignon sizzled on barbecues while drinks appropriately reverted back to red wine. If your appetite isn't satisfied yet, 350 pounds of cheese, pâté, and crackers were served not far from the finish.

Hard-core runners are considered gauche, so much so that the website states: "Spoilsports, thugs, and record seekers are not invited." If you're willing to lighten up you'll blend in, especially if you dress up. Three-quarters of the runners wear elaborate costumes.

Ten-person caterpillars who were literally joined at the hip transformed wine tasting and rest stops into team efforts. Eight toga-clad men carried a stretcher with a Cleopatra character who wisely had cup holders installed. I passed 50 men from Le Mans in straw hats and Victorian bathing suits carrying a beach cabana, runner inside. Time is simply not an issue.

There are few concerns about mixing drinking and running—perhaps because there's no pressure to finish the race. France also enjoys a less litigious society if a mishap occurs. Red Cross tents, usually reserved for competitors suffering from exhaustion, blisters, and pulled hamstrings, were packed with runners receiving mid-race massages. If you'd like to rid yourself of that haggard look from marathon running, a beautician sits not far from the finish to freshen-up your makeup for your victory photo.

Those compelled to cross the finish line receive a generous postrace package. I was handed a gym bag, wood-encased bottle of wine, a rose, and a kiss. The party continued at a recovery area that included more massages, lawn chairs looking out on the estuary, and for those who had some moves left after running 26.2 miles, dancing to live music.

Unconventional marathon ways begin at the pasta party which, like the race, is sold out months in advance. Under a tent adjacent to a grand château, the atmosphere is more reminiscent of a dinner party. Tablecloth dining is de rigueur; long group tables are set with china, flatware, and enough wineglasses to crowd out the bread baskets. Paper plates and plastic forks would simply lend the wrong tone. A wooden dance floor beckons runners to celebrate. A loud, lively band coaxes competitors from worrying about resting their legs.

Menu cards announce the multicourse feast served by uniformed waiters who pour and constantly replenish wine from six-bottle baskets. The scene is set for international dining companions to become friends even if they don't speak the same language.

Competitors come from Europe and beyond, although

runners from France remain the dominant entry. The race sells out months in advance, but 20 percent of the field is reserved for runners outside of the country. Tour operators package the trip with a guaranteed race number, but it's easy and more economical to register yourself. Medical clearance from a doctor is required for registration. A health symposium for doctors takes place in conjunction with the race with seminar topics including "Meat and Long-Distance Running."

The small town of Pauillac has limited hotel rooms. Reserve well in advance, especially if you want to stay at Cordeillan-Bages, a Relais & Châteaux property, or one of the other hotels. Some runners board with local families; not only do they enhance the cultural exchange, it's convenient and much less expensive. Another often-used option is Bordeaux, a city an hour to the south with ample hotels, but requiring a long drive to the race start. Further indulgence in wine country lifestyle is vinothérapie, a wine spa at La Source de Caudalie in nearby Martillac. Treatments using the skins and seeds of grapes result in applications named Merlot Wrap, Wine Barrel Bath, or Crushed Cabernet Scrub.

If you need to recuperate the day after the race, a recovery walk or mountain bike ride through châteaux vineyards is available. Wine and food are included, of course.

LIKE WINE?

Marathon du Médoc is impossible to duplicate, but if you enjoy the idea of running through vineyards that produce a fine glass of wine, try www.destinationraces.com for races in California. They showcase the Napa-to-Sonoma

Wine Country Half-Marathon, Santa Barbara Wine Country Half-Marathon, and Healdsburg Wine Country Half-Marathon, during the summer and fall.

On the U.S. East Coast, there's the Wineglass Marathon (www.wineglassmarathon.com) in Corning, New York, in October. Both marathoners and relay teams crossing the finish receive prizes. Appropriately, it's a bottle of Pleasant Valley New York State Brut Champagne and a unique handmade glass medallion crafted by Hands-on-Glass, a local glass studio.

Fancy a shorter distance and more time enjoying grapes? The XTERRA Boordy Vineyards Scramble 5K, outside of Baltimore, Maryland, starts early on an August evening and finishes with wine, cheese, and music at sunset. Registration is available at www.xterraplanet.com.

THE "ORIGINAL" BARE BUNS FUN RUN
Run Naked

LOCATION: KANIKSU RANCH NUDIST PARK, LOON LAKE,
  WASHINGTON

MONTH: JULY

DISTANCE/AVERAGE FIELD: 3.1 MILES/300

TELEPHONE: 509-327-NUDE (6833)

WEBSITE: www.kaniksufamily.com

Is it contradictory to get a race T-shirt at the Bare Buns Fun Run, when it's held in a nudist colony? This informal event in the Cascade Mountain forest, 40 miles north of Spokane, Washington, is run without tank tops, shorts, or running bras. Get the picture? Naked. But it still requires sneakers so runners can cross electronic timing mats. Maybe deciding where to attach a chip would introduce too many questions.

Actually, clothing is optional, so you don't have to run nude if you don't want to, although participants who may be on the fence are warned that there will be many nude participants and course marshals—you may never look at another race official in the same way again.

If you do decide to jump in the nude pool, don't expect to record the run for your photo album. Cameras, video recording equipment, and digital imaging devices of any kind are not allowed and will be confiscated. Split times are called 1 and 2 miles out, and a half-mile before the end of the race. The course includes a turnaround. Whether you're at the front or the back of the pack, when you see a mass of people running toward you naked, even the most composed runners report getting a little unnerved.

There are numerous age groups, ranging from "5-years-old and under" to "70 and over," and winners are split into male and female, and clothed, nude, and wheelchair divisions. Even the T-shirts announce whether you are simply a "finisher" or—the real deal—"nude finisher." To order the correct clothing quantities, you're asked whether you intend to run nude on the registration form. Although this decision is not binding on race day, it's going to be pretty obvious which T-shirt you'll be awarded.

Water and aid stations are on the course, which is

convenient since water bottle holders strapped to bare waists can cause chafing. The county fire district staffs aid stations and never seems to do a lot of arm twisting to get volunteers.

The entry form states that this is a USA Track & Field-sanctioned event, although it doesn't say whether any of the governing body has participated in the race. It's okay to arrive at the nudist colony entrance clothed, and strip down later. A combination for the lock on the gate for race week is provided on the form. You're asked not to wander off the property in the buff to avoid scaring neighbors.

Campgrounds are available for the weekend if you'd like to bring a tent or RV. Hookups to electricity and water are available for a fee. A carbo-load party is held the night before, at the clubhouse, with a dance afterward. There's no mention whether it's fast or slow music.

Cool morning temperatures in the mountains on race morning convince many to wear warm-up gear and strip down later. Race numbers, attached with a piece of string or yarn, are worn wherever you like (some find it convenient to utilize body piercings). Organizers recommend liberally applying suntan lotion, especially for those parts of your body that aren't used to direct rays. Many participants powder up before the race because running "bare buns" is more conducive to chafing.

Walkers and runners have separate starts, although both include a diverse crowd of runners. Body shapes include skinny and fat. Some runners are young, but most are over 50 years old with a pretty even split between men and women. Those who've indulged say there are a fair number of people they'd prefer to see clothed instead of naked, but chalk it up to freedom of expression. Some people convince a friend to join them whose imperfect naked body makes them feel better about their own.

Although this is a fun run, some participants clock a sub-6-minute-mile. Based on finishing times it's unclear whether the nude runners enjoy an advantage by leaving the weight of clothing behind.

A few runners wait until right before the finish to strip off their clothes. It isn't clear whether this qualifies them for the coveted "Nude Finisher" T-shirt. A postrace party with outdoor activities includes swimming and volleyball. Apparently, this race has competition; several other nude fun runs exist in Portland, Vancouver, and Snoqualmie in Washington. Maybe there's something compelling about running in the buff in the forests out west.

GIVE PEACE A CHANCE

Running around the world provides the chance to see how other people live outside a typical tourist experience. Pasta-party menus featuring traditional dishes of dal bhat or lo mein give you a taste of what locals have for dinner. Landmarks on a course offer a way to appreciate the history others have experienced, as well as give thought to the place that you call home.

Sharing laughs and long conversations with competitors from many different cultures opens windows on how a person on the opposite side of the world lives and struggles day to day, like you. Runners have a forum, a race, that allows people without political agendas to meet. It's a gift.

Competitions in this chapter celebrate coming together for a sporting event. Simply sharing what kind of sneakers each other wears can bridge the growing gap between cultures.

Races within this section also remind us of the destruction history has recorded when competition overrides humanity.

Enjoying heartfelt hospitality extended by strangers when you're far away from home adds comfort and builds confidence that civilians strive for a peaceful place to enjoy friends and family, despite a turbulent world. Lifelong friendships have formed at races and brought people from opposite camps together faster than formal diplomacy. Allowing this sport to continue to build relationships, especially as the popularity of racing grows, is a goal every runner can aim for beyond crossing the finish line.

CONTINENTAL AIRLINES
INTERNATIONAL FRIENDSHIP RUN
United Nations

LOCATION: NEW YORK, NEW YORK

MONTH: NOVEMBER

DISTANCE/AVERAGE FIELD: 2.5 MILES/15,000

TELEPHONE: 212-423-2249

WEBSITE: www.ingnycmarathon.org

The United Nations towers above a starting line packed with runners waving scores of flags from around the world, and outfitted in athletic wear proudly representing their country's colors. This fun run, the day before the New York

City Marathon, is a testament to global good fellowship. Originally a warm-up race available only to the marathon's international entrants, recently this non-timed 2.5-miler around Manhattan has been expanded to include Americans and non-marathoners.

Scores of runners are grouped by their country of origin because they've arrived with friends and loved ones. Those who've traveled here solo can easily join fellow citizens. Compatriots are identifiable from afar because they are waving their country's flag, or wearing T-shirts and jackets adorned with running club mottos in their native language.

A cacophony of languages from all over the world can be heard when you weave through the crowd or if the wind shifts on this fall morning. The change in dialects is as swift and plentiful as scanning music on the radio.

Group costumes are popular at European races, as is dressing up for this celebratory U.S. event. International acquaintances are facilitated by fun-loving accessories, which prove good conversation starters. I have witnessed runners from Amsterdam don bright orange jackets, leggings, and headbands with bobbing antennae sporting twin lion heads resembling Tony the Tiger. A Japanese man led 64 fellow countrymen through the course with music speakers strapped to his waist, playing "We Are the World." Norwegians proudly imitated their flag, painting their faces blue with a white cross traveling chin to forehead and cheek to cheek. Even a little cross-culture dressing has been in evidence. An Italian wore a Japanese robe and headband and carried a toy Samurai sword, with a T-shirt underneath that read "Italia." The excitement inherent the day before a big race runs like electricity through the happy crowd, with a lot of singing and photography taking place.

A horn-blast start sends runners due west, smack through midtown. Running faster than traffic, a liberating feeling sets in as you recall your slow creeping taxi rides, block after block with the meter ticking, on the very same streets.

The course, which crosses 42nd Street and passes Grand Central Terminal, the New York Public Library, and Bryant Park, offers out-of-towners a city tour. Seizing photo opportunities, runners carrying compact cameras ask cohorts to pose for pictures in front of these New York City landmarks. Cameras are often handed off to strangers willing to take a shot so the owner can pose with fellow countrymen, and even convince passing runners to join them for the memory. The double-wide cross street gives ample room for photo ops, large contingents of patriotic runners, and revelers in the sold-out race. Most athletes aren't in a hurry; they're saving their strength for marathon day.

Turning north on 6th Avenue just after Bryant Park, the course passes the International Center of Photography, Rockefeller Center, and Radio City Music Hall. The route steers left onto Central Park South, following the last half mile of the New York City Marathon. Runners get a taste of the merciless incline left for the end of the 26.2-mile race the next day, and relief sets in when the course turns into Central Park with the finish line in sight.

The fun run ends just shy of the marathon finish line, marked by a sign in six different languages. People hug one another, trade their country's flags, and leave in search of restaurants serving breakfast. The crowd is very friendly, whether or not they speak English. You can find yourself either the new owner of an orange headband with antennae lion heads, invited to breakfast, or both. There's no postrace gathering, and the hungry crowd quickly disperses.

Avoiding overexertion is best before a marathon, and the Big Apple provides plenty of nonstrenuous entertainment, from Saturday matinees on Broadway to cruises around Manhattan, to fill the rest of the day. Over 15,000 people, from more than 100 countries, on a casual run celebrating the sport of running is a colorful, friendly, feel-good experience that's well worth joining.

IN FLANDERS FIELDS MARATHON
Where Poppies Grow

LOCATION: FLANDERS, BELGIUM
MONTH: SEPTEMBER
DISTANCE/AVERAGE FIELD: 26.2 MILES/700

TELEPHONE: (Belgium) +32-51-503-129
WEBSITE: www.marathons.be/nl/

In Flanders Fields" is a famous war poem written by John McCrae, a Canadian officer and doctor at the front lines of World War I, in 1915. He was mourning the death of a dear friend and student, Alexis Helmer. Often read by soldiers and civilians who had lost loved ones during the war, the heartfelt verses came to epitomize the senseless loss of life.

Mounting casualties so overwhelmed burial plots in the Flanders battlefields in northern Belgium that tens of thousands of those serving in the military have no known grave, including Helmer. To this day soldiers' remains are uncovered in spring when farmers plow their fields. In Flanders Fields Marathon runs through these historic battlefields, past war monuments and military cemeteries, in the name of peace and remembrance of the suffering in war.

The flat course begins in Nieuwpoort, a seaport on the northern coast of Belgium, 120 kilometers northwest of Brussels. Diverse nationalities are attracted to the race, some of whom have a personal attachment such as a grandparent or great-grandparent who fought or lived in the war-torn region.

The first female American winner ran in honor of her recently deceased grandmother, who lost her brother, house, and ultimately her homeland in Flanders, fleeing Belgium for the United States. Throughout the race, the runner's head was filled with her grandmother's stories about hiding from German soldiers, scrounging for food, and enduring the overwhelming sounds of gunfire and fighter planes filling the air.

During her stay she looked for long-lost relatives or family friends since her grandmother's obliterated village had been located close by. It was the center of the Belgian heritage her grandmother had loved and passed down to her granddaughter. During the search and describing her mission to fellow runners, new friends were made.

The marathon heads south along the Ijzer River beside the sluice, or canals, that were the site of some of the war's fiercest battles. These waterways were strategically utilized to flood the plains to thwart the German advance. Trenches dug nearby held hundreds of thousands of young soldiers from Belgium, France, Ireland, England, Australia, New Zealand, and the United States, to fortify the Allies' position.

Soldiers named holes dug near Diksmuide "death trenches" because they were built without protection from enemy fire and were situated directly across from German fortifications. Battles here resulted in some of the war's worst carnage. Their remnants still exist today and line the race course for miles. Soldier memorials, including the Yser Towers and PAX Gate, offer thoughtful reflection during the race.

Shortly after the start, it's not uncommon for cyclists to join runners en route, offering encouragement, water, and food. Since the field is small and the race informal, cyclists aren't restricted on the course, although some runners find it disconcerting. On Europe's northern coast, changing weather patterns are common, with unexpected swift winds and rain that can douse runners for miles.

The last stretch of the race enters the enchanting town of Ieper-Ypres (Ieper is the Flemish name), where little evidence remains of the complete destruction it suffered, detailed in museum exhibitions and historic photographs on the marathon website. At the finish, after a personal handshake from the race director, runners are treated to Belgian specialties: chocolate and beer.

Currently, there is no transportation back to the starting area at Nieuwpoort. One visiting runner put his luggage on the baggage truck along with his postrace gear, and picked them up at the finish before heading back to Brussels.

"In Flanders Fields" speaks of the poppies that grew between the rows of crosses marking soldiers' graves. Poppies still grace the fields lining the race course and the front of the finishers' medal. The spirit of the competition is similar to what bonded soldiers together to fight the relentless war. Group victory is more important than personal survival. The race is held to raise awareness of the useless violence and terror inherent in war.

> In Flanders fields the poppies blow
> Between the crosses, row on row,
> That mark our place; and in the sky
> The larks, still bravely singing, fly
> Scarce heard amid the guns below.
>
> We are the Dead. Short days ago
> We lived, felt dawn, saw sunset glow,
> Loved, and were loved, and now we lie
> In Flanders fields.
>
> Take up our quarrel with the foe:
> To you from failing hands we throw
> The torch; be yours to hold it high.
> If ye break faith with us who die
> We shall not sleep, though poppies grow
> In Flanders fields.
>
> —JOHN MCCRAE

RUNNING IN REMEMBRANCE

The second oldest marathon in the world, the Košice Peace Marathon was first held in 1924. Run in October, the race now includes a half-marathon, mini-marathon, and 4.2K (2.6 miles). It has continuously been run but for a two-year break during the occupation of Košice, Slovakia, during World War II: www.kosicemarathon.com/en.

- -

INTERNATIONAL PEACE MARATHON OF KIGALI
Rwanda's New Course

LOCATION: KIGALI, RWANDA

MONTH: MAY

DISTANCE/AVERAGE FIELD: 26.2 MILES/150, 13.1 MILES/800, 3.1 MILES/1,000

TELEPHONE: (Rwanda) +250-511802

WEBSITE: www.kigalimarathon.com

- -

Rwanda's name still invokes memories of the 1994 genocide, resulting in an estimated one million deaths from Rwandan-on-Rwandan violence. The International Peace Marathon in the capital of Kigali seeks to promote reconciliation from this devastating period, when the Tutsi minority suffered the most at the hands of the Hutu majority. The mission of the race is to rebuild ties and strengthen social development torn apart in the aftermath of the civil war. It's only been a few years since the 2005 inaugural run, but to show support runners have come from Europe, North America, and Australia to join elite runners from 10 African countries.

Spectators are plentiful in this east-central African nation of 9 million people, the most densely populated country on the continent. Enthusiastic schoolchildren will run with you for miles at a time. There's little concept of personal space as they tug at your arm, shirt, or shorts, even wanting to hold hands for a group run. Running buddies aren't limited to children. It's not unheard of for African runners to "adopt" visiting competitors and keep pace for the duration of the race.

Between the hilly course, hot sun, and the altitude, this is not an easy race. Temperatures feel more intense than the 80 degrees Fahrenheit reached on a course offering little shade, although morning temperatures can dip lower by 20 degrees. At 5,512 feet, the altitude adds to the challenge, as does a four-loop course that includes a 1,149-foot climb. Runners who've finished other marathons such as New York, London, and Chicago report not being able to finish this race. DNFs (did not finish) have been as high as 25 percent of the field.

Checkpoints stock fruit, Coke, sponges, and water. Although you'll be thirsty enough to grab the paper cups, remember not to drink the water if it isn't bottled. To ensure sanitary water and handling standards, bring your own bottled liquids and race food. The laissez-faire organizational style has resulted in late starts. Be prepared to be flexible and self-sufficient, and don't rely on efficient course support. Focusing on the efforts of organizers and participants to build peace and goodwill through sport will provide you with the best race experience.

This peace marathon was initiated by Soroptimist International, an 85-year-old service organization of professional women committed to advancing women's and human rights. Membership spreads across 1,200 clubs in 57 countries. Registration fees, inexpensive compared to many other races, are requested to be wired to a bank in Luxembourg.

A 5K (3.1 mile) Fun Run is held for students selected from all over the country. Many also enter the half-marathon. Schoolchildren run in their street clothes and shoes, or bare feet, since they don't have traditional shorts or sneakers.

The soccer field at Amahoro Stadium provides a wide assortment of constant entertainment for the spectators there to welcome the triumphant runners. Traditional and modern music is played, African and hip-hop dance troupes entertain, even the Rwandan Karate Club members demonstrate their skills. It's all interrupted by applause for each exhausted runner entering the stadium. At the end, race organizers and contributors, ministers, runners, and spectators, hand in hand, run a lap inside the stadium.

THE TUNNEL TO TOWERS RUN
September 11th Fallen Fireman Tribute

LOCATION: NEW YORK, NEW YORK

MONTH: SEPTEMBER

DISTANCE/AVERAGE FIELD: 3.1-MILE RUN/WALK/10,000

TELEPHONE: 718-987-1931

WEBSITE: www.tunneltotowersrun.org

On September 11, Stephen Siller, an off-duty fireman on his way to play golf, turned his truck around to report to work upon hearing that the World Trade Center was attacked. He was stopped on his way to the Brooklyn Battery Tunnel, because he wasn't driving an official vehicle. Grabbing 80 pounds of gear, he ran through the tunnel toward the Towers until a fire truck picked him up. He reached them in time to assist fellow firefighters rescuing civilians. The father of five died inside when the buildings collapsed.

Today, the Tunnel to Towers Run honors Stephen Siller, 343 fallen firefighters, police officers, EMS workers, military personnel, and fellow heroes. The race start can be found in Brooklyn's Red Hook section, among myriad cross streets. Look for crowds, police cars, and signs for the Brooklyn Battery Tunnel.

Runners on the street are quickly swallowed into the tunnel. Splitting into lanes as smoothly as vehicles do, competitors bypass tollbooths, normally lined with cars. Surveying the field my year, I saw a firefighter dressed in full gear run into the tunnel reminiscent of Siller's heroic feat, military personnel dressed in fatigues carrying backpacks, and West Point cadets running in formation.

Semicircled with shiny white tile, Brooklyn Battery Tunnel is thoroughly cleaned in anticipation of the race. Carbon monoxide lingering from vehicles is pumped out either side, which can leave the interior actually smelling like fresh air. On a humid day, packed with runners, it can get sticky inside, prompting you to keep looking for the light at the end of the tunnel. The underwater transverse winds its way under the East River for 1.7 miles before arriving at Manhattan's doorstep, where the World Trade Center towers once stood.

In honor of Siller and others who died that fateful day, firefighting companies stand just outside the Manhattan exit applauding and cheering participants. Attired in work duty uniform, some men grip polished dark wood poles carrying the American flag, others hold pictures and honor rolls of their comrades who perished at the scene.

This is an emotional race. Runners and firefighters have tears in their eyes, thinking back to loved ones, and even strangers, who lost their lives that day. Participants include firefighters' families and friends from all across the country, as well as honor contingents from the 82nd Airborne Division, Navy SEALs, Marine Corps Recon, and other military representation. All runners are welcome, and can register beforehand or on site.

Exiting the tunnel on the Manhattan side, runners head toward neighboring World Financial Center, a complex of high-rise office buildings and stores. In recent years, a celebratory atmosphere has crept into the race as participation has swelled. Cheerleaders and high school bands are now entertaining runners on the sidelines. The scenic promenade up the Hudson River boat basin, dotted with sailboats and yachts, is part of the route. Runners pass the Winter Garden, a glass-enclosed atrium on the water. Circling back to the finish line on West Street, the course ends where the World Trade Center once shadowed lower Manhattan. It's now the construction site for the National September 11 Memorial & Museum at the World Trade Center and the 1,776-foot-tall Freedom Tower.

A postrace party offers sumptuous food and one of the most bountiful buffets ever found after a race. Grilled chicken, steak, sweet sausages, pasta, and other entrées are served by vendors lining the double-wide street. Beverages from beer to lemonade are available. Pies, brownies, and more sweet tooth–satisfying desserts are in store.

Several bands play for the crowds. Sand sculpture artists create life-sized tributes to firemen, the Towers, and the race. Family entertainment includes face painting for children.

The race is a fund-raiser for the Stephen Siller, FDNY, "Let Us Do Good" Children's Foundation. The nonprofit supports burn centers throughout the U.S. and community services that help children who have lost one or more parents. In addition to paying tribute to local heroes, the race celebrates life, as we so often forget to do.

HIT THE BEACH

For some runners, the sun and surf make their day. Racing beside a white sandy beach, grateful for the cool breeze off the water, is their idea of paradise. Or, ending the run with a dip in the ocean is incentive enough to register for a race.

If sandy scenery is your personal choice, there are many races worth the trip and the sunblock. Creative competitions take place from the windswept beaches of the North Atlantic coast to tropical islands in the South Pacific.

There's a long-distance race run barefoot on a beach—a course your feet will never forget. Water-filled trenches and man-made dunes are among the race hazards. Runners must also be careful of tripping and skinning their knees, or not closing their eyes when competitors kick up sand.

Other favorite coastal scenes have tens of thousands of devoted followers, and a race field resembling a beach party rather than an athletic event. You'll have to maneuver around parade floats resembling a 2-story Trojan horse, a jet plane complete with flight attendants and a luggage carousel belt, and other creative assemblies. If your running time is paramount, take your mark near the race start, before the frivolous masses.

Running on beaches may help keep you cool, but it doesn't reduce the amount of water your body needs to remain hydrated. If the aid stations along the course are infrequent, carry plenty of your own water. Before the race, apply a generous amount of a high-SPF waterproof sunblock, which helps prevent sweat from dissolving the lotion on your skin on shade-deprived courses.

Whether you favor a traditional road race near the smell of a saltwater ocean, or a movable party disguised as a run, courses on the sandy side keep your running fun. It's another way to diversify your routine and expand your race experience.

ING BAY TO BREAKERS
San Francisco's Finest

LOCATION: SAN FRANCISCO, CALIFORNIA
MONTH: MAY
DISTANCE/AVERAGE FIELD: 7.5 MILES/65,000+

TELEPHONE: 415-359-2800
WEBSITE: www.ingbaytobreakers.com

Bay to Breakers is more like a traveling party than a road race, unless of course you're an elite runner competing for prize money. But why worry about speed when most of the fun is farther back in the pack? More than 65,000 runners set off from Embarcadero, San Francisco's scenic district on the bay. The masses wind their way up and over one of the city's famous hills before ending in Golden Gate Park, by Ocean Beach, home of the breaking waves that are part of the race's namesake.

Participants of all levels are welcome. Runners veer left and walkers stay to the right during the race, always held the third Sunday in May. You may just want to slow down and take it all in. That's the philosophy of CANKLE, or Citizens Against Needless Kinetic-Led Energy. Their insistence that walking should prevail over running prompts signs that trumpet: YOUR RUNNING DOES NOT IMPRESS ME and WHAT'S THE RUSH?

At a race start jammed with competitors, the field flings tortillas into the air and into fellow runners—a tradition from the 1990s. Legend has it that someone didn't have a beach ball to toss, but he did have several bags of tortillas in his refrigerator that he passed out to friends. The race fad continues, as do the beach balls. Hundreds of multicolored inflated spheres bounce between outstretched arms. T-shirts are also on the list of paraphernalia thrown toward the sky.

Costumes are popular and creative. Two people have run as a pair of hands, each of their heads sticking out one of the five fingers. Cavemen wearing loincloths have been mounted on a homemade wooly mammoth. Inspired by the documentary *March of the Penguins,* the number of runners with beaks, white chests, and wings could populate a rookery. Scrabble pieces have formed words on request, and there's even been a spaghetti-and-meatballs outfit. A Transportation Safety Administration airport screener has been seen running around scanning women with his security wand.

More than a few people choose not to wear anything except sneakers and socks, taking part in the Bare-2-Breakers movement for public acceptance of nudity. There've been requests from clothed runners that future participants refrain from displaying their birthday suits, unless they've been approached by a glamour magazine for a photo shoot.

Parade floats travel with the crowd. Imitations of Neverland Ranch, complete with a look-alike Michael Jackson, compete with a NASCAR pit crew and homemade racing car. A thatched roof tiki bar has been seen driving by, stocked with a half-dozen kegs and bartenders blending margaritas and piña coladas. Security has increased policing the course for alcoholic beverages, which are officially prohibited, as is the aforementioned nudity.

Bay to Breakers is home to the World Centipede Running Championships. Yes, there is such a club for athletes choosing to run in groups of thirteen. Tied together, they're required to perform a Lenichi Turn, a 360-degree circle in Golden Gate Park. Twinkie feelers are required on each head, while a stinger "of appropriate design and toxicity" on the rear runner must touch the remnants of Pier 16 on San Francisco Bay at the race start, according to rules adopted by the International Centipede Congress. Each centipede is checked prior to the race to prevent ineligible starts.

"Spawn" is a long-held tradition. It's a collection of runners dressed like salmon who run "upstream," as salmon do to mate. That means they're required to run the race from finish to start. The school of fish is assembled by "The Cacophony Society" (visit www.cacophony.org), an organization originating in San Francisco dedicated to "free spirits united in the pursuit of experiences beyond the pale of mainstream society." In preparation of yelling "spawn" throughout the race, the school of fish have their own pre-race party, only salmon invited. Their suits are waterproof so they can spawn rain or shine.

At its height in 1986, the event registered 110,000 runners and made the *Guinness Book of World Records* for holding the world's largest footrace. If you've run a marathon with a field of 30,000, picture a race at twice the population with one-third the distance. Translated this means that you are running with a large, compressed, and distracted crowd with many people who've been drinking. Human road hazards are abundant and water stations can be difficult to access simply because of the numbers involved.

Sixteen bands provide entertainment along the course. The celebrations continue under the banner of ING Footstock in Golden Gate Park. Revelers frolic in beer gardens and around a hot-air balloon, and compete in a costume contest. One musical group plays by popular demand, selected at a Battle of the Bands contest held several weeks before the race.

With all the commotion, it's hard to imagine that Bay to Breakers is rooted in turn-of-the-century San Francisco history. After Frisco survived its most destructive earthquake in 1906, events were held to rebuild their morale. Originally named the Cross City Race, the inaugural affair in 1912 was composed of a field of less than 200 men. Women weren't allowed entry until 1971, although one disguised as a man snuck onto the course 30 years earlier. Renamed Bay to Breakers in 1963, the race has transformed into a world-renowned city celebration. Imagine what the originators would think of their race in the Golden Gate City today.

MANLY WHARF HOTEL SOFT SAND CLASSIC
Quick, Sandy, and Barefoot

LOCATION: MANLY, AUSTRALIA (7 Miles from Sydney)
MONTH: JUNE
DISTANCE/AVERAGE FIELD: 13 MILES/60, 5.6 MILES/225, 1 MILE/50

TELEPHONE: (Australia) +61-2-9977-2742
WEBSITE: www.manlylsc.com

Lifeguards at one of Sydney's best-known resorts tell runners to hit the beach in the Soft Sand Classic, a run held entirely on sand, sponsored by the Manly Life Saving Club. Pounding your feet into a soft surface that constantly gives has its challenges. Most competitors prefer to run barefoot, gripping the grains with their toes and landing on the balls of their feet for optimal traction. The downside to this non-traditional running form is more work for the calves, causing them to cramp up if you're not well-trained.

Veterans draft the leaders, following their tracks, much like in cycling. The front-runners' feet do all the hard work, firming up the surface for those behind them to take advantage of an easier spring from their step. Compacted beach underfoot improves finishing times, so in this race competitors pray for wet weather. Although running in sand has a low-impact advantage that can increase resistance to injuries, it is also far more exhausting. A lack of traction makes it more taxing because a planted foot gets more resistance from a hard ground. Back and shoulders do more work by helping to maintain a weight balance on the uneven beach. But devotees who have mastered the surface say that running with soft, undisturbed sand underfoot creates the same heavenly rhythm as skiing in snow.

The race begins at Manly Beach, the first seaside resort north of Sydney. Four hills of sand are planted on the length of the out-and-back course extending between South Steyne and Queenscliff. There are fourteen lengths run in the 21K (13 miles) event, six lengths for the 9K (5.6 miles) race, and one length for the 1.6K (1 mile) stretch. The 9K event, dubbed the Soft Sand Cup, was introduced several years ago and has become the most popular because of the shorter distance. Those who've completed the 21K course have boasted that it's almost equivalent to a marathon on a flat surface, although the record finishing time isn't comparable, at 1:29:19.

Race proceeds are donated to the Manly Life Saving Club, an organization of lifeguards and water rescue personnel that patrol the beaches. The club was established in 1903, shortly after swimming in the surf in daylight became legal, to prevent drownings. The event was founded in 1993 by Scott Wood and the Manly Council lifeguards. The oceanside resort with its hotels and cafés looks to this popular event to boost business. Local newspapers do their part to lure additional runners by boasting of the breakfast aromas of pancakes and bacon coming off the wharf. No doubt while competitors are trudging through the sand, they're anticipating their well-earned meal.

THE SUN-HERALD CITY2SURF
Sydney's Bay to Breakers

LOCATION: SYDNEY, AUSTRALIA

MONTH: AUGUST

DISTANCE/AVERAGE FIELD: 8.7 MILES/65,000

TELEPHONE: (Australia) +61-2-9282-2833

WEBSITE: http://city2surf.sunherald.com.au

Australians love their sport and their fun. There's no better evidence of it than City2Surf, a 14K (8.7 miles) fun run from Hyde Park to one of Sydney's beloved strips of sand, Bondi Beach. The race got its start when a New York reporter sent *The Sun* (now *The Sun-Herald*) editor an article about San Francisco's famous Bay to Breakers race, in 1970. By the next year, Sydney had an outrageous race of its own, with 2,000 participants.

An hour before the event, streets are flooded with an estimated 65,000 entries. Registered competitors are joined by thousands of unofficial runners who crash the race midway, so they can celebrate at finish-line festivities. Staggered starts accommodate large numbers to such an extent that the later groups can still be at the starting line when the first competitors cross the finish line. No one seems to mind, as runners are laughing, singing, joking, dancing, and casting off their warm-up clothes shortly into the race. Sweatpants, shirts, and jackets left along the road are collected later and donated to charity.

Runners overrun the streets en masse close to the start. Everyone running, headed in one direction, can resemble a movie scene in which the population is fleeing the city. One runner's advice was to register a time for the third wave or above if you think you can run the course in under two hours. Otherwise, participants in later starts will find them-selves navigating family-oriented groups pushing strollers and holding little children's hands.

The course heads into Kings Cross and through a street tunnel splitting into several tubes, so pick a lane. Inside, in-stead of familiar traffic noises, the sound of pounding sneakers fills your ears. Toward Rose Bay, 3 miles into the race, spectators encourage runners by moving their home-stereo speakers to the windowsills, adding their personal taste in music to the affair. Live bands on the course play their song selections, varying from rock and roll to classical music.

Costumes are popular—runners have colored their bod-ies blue, green, or pink with matching running shorts, or dressed up as ATMs or *Idol* judges who are rating the run-ners. Even elaborate dinosaur attire worthy of placement in a natural history museum has dominated the streets.

Strangers often befriend fellow competitors, becoming running partners for long stretches of the race. They even cool off together when spectators turn on their garden hoses to provide participants relief from the heat.

Sydney's scenic eastern harbor comes into view at Rose Bay. Beautiful sailboats crowd the cove. Waterside spectators perched on deck, drink in hand, cheer on runners and occasionally blow air horns. City sights on the horizon such as Harbor Bridge and the Opera House create a postcard-perfect panorama.

The distraction is short-lived when "Heartbreak Hill" comes into view halfway through the course. The mile-long climb challenges more celebratory participants. Many simply choose to walk the incline. Take the hill more aggressively and the finish quickly comes into view. The final stretch along the ocean ends at Bondi Beach, swarmed by a massive sea of people.

Sporting their medals, finishers push their toes in the sand on the ocean strip that's famous for sunning, surfing, and reveling. Participants also receive a certificate and a free copy of *The Sun-Herald* newspaper. Postrace food and partying lasts throughout the day.

There is no cutoff time. A manned finish line stays in place until the last participants straggle through, about $5^1/2$ hours after the race start. Officials don't mind hanging out at the finish to accommodate latecomers at the annual August event. Down Under it's wintertime, but in Sydney that's an average of 64 degrees Fahrenheit, still pleasant weather for a race to the beach.

TAHITI MOOREA MARATHON
Hot Tropical Paradise

LOCATION: MOOREA ISLAND, FRENCH POLYNESIA

MONTH: FEBRUARY

DISTANCE/AVERAGE FIELD: 26.2 MILES/125, 13.1 MILES/325,
    3.1 MILES/144

TELEPHONE: (French Polynesia) +689-466-800

WEBSITE: www.mooreaevents.org

Beating the heat is why the Tahiti Moorea Marathon begins before dawn, but at sunrise, the coastline-hugging course won't let you forget that you're on a tropical island. A 4:30 a.m. start and 9:00 a.m. prize ceremony easily qualify it as one of the earliest marathons in the world. If you scheduled your arrival in the South Pacific close to the race, your jet lag will come in handy when you have to get up in the middle of the night to prepare for the start.

Moorea, next to Tahiti and one of 118 islands comprising French Polynesia, was visited by Captain Cook, the eighteenth-century British explorer. Rumor has it he destroyed canoes and houses after locals refused to return a stolen goat—back then island residents had no concept of ownership. Such a unique sensibility may have something to do with the heat. When the sun rises, temperatures can reach 90 degrees Fahrenheit. Couple that with high humidity and there's little relief from the balmy South Pacific Ocean breezes.

The marathon, half-marathon, and 5K (3.1 miles) races take

place on the same day in February, during French Polynesia's summer. The seasonal average rainfall reaches 10 inches a month, twice Seattle's monthly winter average. There's a good chance that you'll be running on a wet, cloudy day.

Exotic scenery can take your mind off the heat. Lush, green volcanic mountains divide Moorea into eight ridges. The marathon course winds its way around four of them with sky-blue lagoons lining the coastal road race course.

Organizers have increased the number of water stations to every 2.5K, but given the high humidity you may still want to run with your own bottle. Tahitian music from traditional instruments such as pahu tupa'e and other drums are played, while liquids are handed out at the aid stations. Sunscreen is essential because the course is almost totally exposed to sunlight. Even if it's overcast, it's easy to burn. The finish line and postrace party in a beachside tent serves up fruit, bread, peanut butter, and Nutella. Bring a towel so you can jump into the ocean to cool off.

EasyTahiti.com, a travel service, offers to book race packages including air fare, ferry transfers, hotel, and marathon entry. They advertise that their staff will even join you in the race, the caveat being how well their training program is going. You may want to remain flexible, too, and run a shorter distance if you're not a hot-weather runner.

Tahitian fire dancers tossing knives, dressed in grass skirts and colorful native flower leis, entertain you at the prerace pasta party on Temae Beach. Dishes include exotic fruit and pineapple, Moorea's main agricultural product. Seafood pasta served with locally caught fish will help you carbo-load with a South Pacific flair.

A range of celebrations around the marathon are held all weekend long, including canoe races and fashion shows. The day after the marathon, if your feet have not cooled off, there's an "Umu Ti," or "walking on fire" performance. In what must be the most unique race feature of all time, runners are invited to remove their sneakers and walk barefoot over red-hot coals. You may prefer to simply lie on the beach.

LIKE BEACHES?

If your favorite course is sun and sand, don't forget Brazil's famous beaches. Information about the Rio Marathon races in June (the Southern Hemisphere's winter) is at www.maratonadorio.com.br.

LISTEN TO THE MUSIC

What is it about a song that can seamlessly divert a runner's focus from physical fatigue to physical exertion? The same reason a rhythm can entice you to dance; it motivates you to stick out that mile, tapping a special reserve of physical energy, especially when you hear your favorite tunes.

When music became portable, it changed the pace of running forever. Transistor radios first allowed you to take music on the run. Walkmans with cassette players, and now iPods and other MP3 players, enhanced the experience by creating the ability to pair your running rhythm with inspirational songs.

Now each stage of your run can warrant musical variation, from warming up, to achieving a stride, then hitting a sprint. Genres ranging from pop to rock 'n' roll to techno can be woven in, layered with select bands and favorite songs. Sharing carefully composed lists with running buddies and friends has become a pre- and postrace ritual.

The bond formed with personalized music has become so strong, it's addictive. Those armed with iPods and headphones may refuse to run without them. Protesting purists say that a head filled with music shuts out ambient noise from cars, cyclists, park dwellers, and especially Mother Nature. They feel that it interferes with running, or at least the safety of the sport. But, whether or not you run with music channeled to your ears, you can't deny the magical qualities of songs and how they enhance pounding the pavement.

It wasn't a far stretch, then, for music to be featured at running events. Races increasingly amplified tunes that not only made runners feel good, but matched the locale or gave the race a personality. From opera in Italy to country music in Nashville, races in this section serenade runners throughout the race, throughout the world. It energizes not only competitors. All along the course, songs enhance the experience of volunteers and spectators, and add a unique, exciting aspect to those all-too-familiar miles.

COUNTRY MUSIC MARATHON & HALF-MARATHON
Music City

LOCATION: NASHVILLE, TENNESSEE

MONTH: APRIL

DISTANCE/AVERAGE FIELD: 26.2 MILES/6,000, 13.1 MILES/26,000

TELEPHONE: 800-311-1255

WEBSITE: www.cmmarathon.com

Heartbreaking hills, burning pain, tears of joy. Feelings ignited by long-distance running are amazingly similar to a country music song. What better way to endure the agony and ecstasy of extreme physical exertion, mile after mile, than hearing lyrics that you can relate to? At least, that's the attraction for 32,000 participants at the Nashville Country Music Marathon and Half-Marathon. They forget their aches and pain with the help of fifty local bands, playing along a course that winds its way through the heart of Music City.

Musicians volunteering for this daylong gig just might get their big break. Songs striking a chord with runners and spectators may be noticed by someone who works in the music industry. John Rich and Big Kenny, once regulars at the finish, are now known as Big & Rich, with hits including "Save a Horse (Ride a Cowboy)." Julie Roberts and Dierks Bentley are also Country Music Marathon alumni. Some bands are already familiar to veteran runners and spectators, having played annually since the inaugural race in 2000.

Musicians hoping to entertain runners submit a CD to race

organizers. Artists are selected for one of the twenty-eight stages, each assigned two bands that trade off, so no one has to play for six straight hours. Popular, upbeat songs are encouraged. They can be played repeatedly since the audience continually changes, unless an injury stops you in your tracks. Then that tune may become one that you never want to hear again.

Melodies aren't limited to country. Jazz, rock and roll, swing, and other sounds will keep your feet moving toward the finish line. Country Music Television even comes to the race, erecting its own entertainment stage between mile 1 and mile 2.

Just in case the music doesn't see you through, 1,500 cheerleaders armed with pom-poms, megaphones, and chants entertain from twenty-one dedicated stages of their own. They are enthusiastic high school students cooking up ways to encourage runners, part of a course-wide contest awarding prizes for the best routines.

Both the marathon and much larger half-marathon field start at Centennial Park near the Parthenon. The full-scale replica of the Athens temple houses one of Nashville's art museums. Runners' split times at three intervals for the half-marathon and five for the full marathon, and are recorded online. Live results are posted every minute so friends and loved ones near a computer can keep track.

The urban course passes tourist attractions such as Music Row, the heart of Nashville's music industry since the 1950s. Elvis recorded more than 200 hits in studios here. The voices of Garth Brooks, Reba McEntire, Dixie Chicks, and Hilary Duff have also floated through the halls.

Full marathoners report a drop in entertainment and support after the half-marathon splits off. It may not be surprising—half-marathoners make up more than 75 percent of participants, so the best resources are concentrated in the first half of the race. Temperatures, which can zoom well above the advertised average of 60 degrees Fahrenheit, make it tough to master the rolling hills scattered throughout the course. One first-timer described her plight as worse than giving birth to her 9-pound, 6-ounce boy without pain medication.

Closer to the finish at LP Field, home of the Tennessee Titans, the entertainment picks up again and there's more music to take your mind off your blisters, as well as ample food and drink. After you hit the showers, if you're still up for more, there's an evening concert with headline entertainment that extends postrace partying well into the night.

MARATONA DELLE TERRE VERDIANE (VERDI'S MARATHON)
A Day at the Opera

LOCATION: SALSOMAGGIORE TERME, ITALY

MONTH: FEBRUARY

DISTANCE/AVERAGE FIELD: 26.2 MILES/700, 19.1 MILES/700,
   14 MILES/400, 6.2 MILES/300

TELEPHONE: (Italy) +39-052-457-2083

WEBSITE: www.verdimarathon.it

Powerful music and drama laced throughout an opera is compelling, but if it's difficult for you to sit still through a three-hour performance, try running to it instead. "Maratona delle Terre Verdiane" translates to "Marathon in the Land of Verdi"—Giuseppe Verdi, that is, one of Italy's most important composers who scored *Aida, Rigoletto,* and other world-renowned Romantic Era nineteenth-century operas.

Four races ranging from 6.2 to 26.2 miles travel through five Italian villages, while *Forces of Destiny* and Verdi's other well-known works are played through stereo speakers. Races begin in Salsomaggiore Terme, a town in Northern Italy celebrated for therapeutic waters thought to cure bronchial and gastric problems, and home to the Miss Italy beauty pageant.

Runners are led through the countryside of the Emilia-Romagna region, about 70 miles southeast of Milan, celebrated the world over for Parmigiano-Reggiano cheese. The 10K (6.2 mile) race finishes in Fidenza, a village known for Domninus of Fidenza, a twelfth-century cathedral named after the martyr. Out front, a statue of the apostle Simon Peter points south. He holds a card reading "I show you the way to Rome," one of the world's first road signs. Runners in the longer-distance races are pointed east instead. They pass Fidenza Village, a shopping outlet proudly marked on the course map, and a race sponsor, along with the Parmigiano-Reggiano cheese consortium.

Most of the route is farmland road, rich with aromas from wheat and grass, grown to feed the cows that make the cheese. Local cheese, fresh fruit, and accompaniments are served throughout the race. The 14-miler finish line is in Fontanellato; 19.1-milers continue to Soragna, about 3 miles shy of Verdi's birthplace in Roncole. Amplifiers hoisted on cars keep music flowing on those 6-mile stretches between towns. Arias such as "La Donna e Mobile" ("Women Are Fickle") fill the air, sung by Pavarotti, Domingo, Lanza, Caruso, and other world-famous tenors.

Marathoners reach Roncole at mile 21. At one time Verdi's birthplace was an inn. Today the building is a tourist attraction sporting a bust of the composer out front. Runners pass by here and Saint Michael's Church where Verdi was baptized and played the organ as a young child.

Despite celebrated arias and legendary compositions, such as "Morir! Tremenda Cosa!" ("To Die! A Terrible Thing!") playing throughout the course, some runners still prefer listening to their own music. A few years ago the ubiquitous iPod ignited a movement to ban MP3 players for disregarding the tribute to the great composer. It's since been decided to allow such devices, but it would be a shame to travel all this way and not pay homage to Verdi.

The marathon finish is in Busetto, where the composer grew up and returned to become town music master after studying in Milan. There he fell in love with and married his sponsor's daughter, Margherita. She gave birth to two children who died in infancy, before she herself passed away at a young age. Verdi was devastated and vowed to give up music forever. Instead, he was convinced to write his second opera, *Nabucco*, in 1842. Its opening performance made him famous.

The pasta party is worthy of its Italian namesake, with a variety of noodle shapes and homemade sauces. The celebration is well attended by locals who give a warm welcome to international entrants. Several years ago, when two American women arrived at the dinner to register, the race director suddenly appeared with a microphone. He announced their arrival to the crowd, noting the long distance they had traveled. Showered with applause, they were presented with matching gifts of a massive cheese wedge and knife in a decorative box. After flying home, friends consumed the cheese over a period of several months, but fond memories of the race, and the gift, linger to this day.

REGGAE MARATHON & HALF-MARATHON
We Be Jammin'

LOCATION: NEGRIL, JAMAICA

MONTH: DECEMBER

DISTANCE/AVERAGE FIELD: 26.2 MILES/200, 13.1 MILES/600,
6.2 MILES/250

TELEPHONE: (Jamaica) 876-922-8677

WEBSITE: www.reggaemarathon.com

When better to run than in the Caribbean in the middle of winter? That was the theory of the Jamdammers, members of the local Jamaican running club. First assembled in 1995, an informal gathering of locals showed up for weekly runs at "the dam," the reservoir for Kingston, the country's capital. It grew into a series of races, then the inaugural Reggae Marathon in 2001.

You can run alongside Jamdammers at the Reggae Marathon races, held the first Saturday in December. The finisher's medal proudly displays Oran, the official mascot, his dreadlocks flying in the air, held back by a headband, while slinging a Jamaican flag over his shoulder. To earn one, though, you'll have to rise before dawn.

Early mornings aren't usually associated with reggae bands, but they are with marathons. Live music graces an earlier-than-average race start at 5:15 a.m., so runners can beat the Caribbean heat. Flaming bamboo torches on parade greet bleary-eyed participants, lighting the way toward the starting line at Norman Manley Boulevard, outside Long Bay Beach Park.

The course heads 3 miles south to Negril, a hotel town an hour from Montego Bay, known for all-inclusive resorts such as Sandals. A turnaround routes competitors back past the start on the fairly flat highway, hugging the west coast of the island, to the 10K (6.2 miles), then the half-marathon finish. Marathoners continue several more miles, until a turnaround leads them back to the race start/finish.

The half-marathon and 10K begin so early that you run mostly in the dark. Roads near the start are reported to be a little uneven and difficult to master without light. As the sun rises, runners get a better view. Fishermen on their boats, loaded with nets and pots, head out from the bay to pursue their daily catch. Songs are sung by local schoolchildren standing under palm trees. Bands and some entrepreneurial performers entertain athletes, but not as often as expected. Cars blaring reggae music pick up where the bands leave off, to serenade you for the duration of the race.

Scenery is spectacular when you get past the hotels and vegetation. Ocean views open up about a quarter of the way into the race, revealing the turquoise blue Caribbean waters. Powdery, fine white sand beaches, once a haven for flower children and hippies in the 1960s, stretch for miles. It keeps you fantasizing about your postrace dip. On the opposite side of the road, cows and goats graze near the villages.

Runners, in the past, especially in the marathon, have shared the road with cars, buses, and motorbikes. Tailpipe exhaust was disconcerting, but now organizers say that they're closing the roads to all but official vehicles. At the far end of the course, there are fewer runners and spectators, and the villages are very poor.

Hydrating requires a different way of downing fluids than drinking from a bottle or a cup. Volunteers hand out water and energy drinks in tightly sealed plastic bags, which you grab, tear open with your teeth, and suck down your throat. The method leaves a fair amount of liquid on your shirt and dribbling down your arms. The packaging can still be convenient for dousing your overheated head or chest.

Hot, humid conditions culminate as the sun rises overhead on a course with little shade. Temperatures easily reach 80 degrees Fahrenheit and 90 percent humidity, increasing the importance of the water stations found every mile. Ice in plastic bags or wrapped in towels proves essential for cooling off, as do misters, spray bottles filled with water.

Sweaty, exhausted runners hitting the wall are heartened when schoolchildren supply energy drinks, gels, and water from their private stashes. Volunteers are enthusiastic and plentiful, representing all walks of life. One group that escorted an athlete to the end of the race included an ambulance, a volunteer on a bike, and a policeman. Once, a driver in a car equipped with a sound system playing reggae followed an injured runner from mile 19 to the finish. When the grateful runner turned to thank the driver, he had already driven off to find his next prospect, no doubt. Children often run or pedal their bikes alongside you. Such kindnesses make this a great event for slower marathoners and walkers who feel that support fades as finishing times lengthen.

Rastafarians are among the many volunteers, standing out with heads full of uncombed dreadlocks. They are members of a movement that grew in Jamaica in the 1930s because of poor living conditions and a belief that smoking ganja (marijuana) enhances greater communication with God.

In Jamaican style, runners are handed a beer at the finish. If you don't like alcohol at the end of a race, coconuts sliced open with a machete will supply you with fresh milk. Postrace massages and bananas are also available, but many seeking relief from the heat dive straight into the ocean.

Marathon winners are awarded prizes reggae-style. The first man and woman across the finish line take home, respectively, the Bob Marley Trophy, a cast of the singer sporting dreadlocks and a guitar in an onstage pose, and the Rita Marley Trophy, dreadlocked, turbaned, and ready to dance the night away.

The three-day expo at the Couples Swept Away Sporting Complex includes more than the typical running shirts, shorts, and sneakers. Booths are decorated with hand-crafted masks for sale. They sport names like "Red Rebel Woman" or "Knots of Life," with dreadlocks made of coconut-husk hair or palm fronds. Then, of course, there's Jamaican rum cake. If you catch "the fever" you can enhance your race-day outfit by purchasing a necklace or bracelet made of shells, not an uncommon sight at the race start.

The pasta party gets very high marks. Chefs from Negril's top resorts hold a cooking competition at a variety of food stations more suggestive of a Caribbean wedding than a carbo-loading dinner. Tents are adorned with tropical flowers and elaborately carved fruit and ice sculptures. Although in the past, registrations at the race expo have been accepted, race-day registrations are not. Sign up in advance if you want to be jammin'.

Rock 'n' Roll Races
HEAVY MEDAL SERIES

If music is your passion and rock and roll is your beat, here's a series of runs that will convince you to leave your iPod at home. Eight races across the country, including new races in Chicago and Seattle in 2009, stage musical groups every mile, lending a partylike atmosphere to pounding the pavement. Cheering squads pipe in with routines to convince you to never give up—prepare to be singled out if you wear your name on your shirt. Water stops are manned by costumed volunteers dressed as pirates, rock stars, and superheroes, and in drag, to name a few genres. Then, of course, there's a postrace party.

The celebration built around the Rock 'n' Roll Marathon series is not to be missed for some, and too commercial for others. An inadequate gel supply or unpopular energy drinks on some courses have turned runners off for good, or simply convinced others to carry their own. Race start access, traffic flow, and parking are tricky and require planning ahead because of large crowds. Arrive extra early to more easily negotiate the tens of thousands of runners and spectators the events draw.

Respectable prize money draws elite running talent like Khalid Khannouchi. News anchors and other local celebrities are also known to lace up their sneakers or make special appearances.

Bands audition for the daylong gig by sending in their press kit (CD, bios, and picture) to the series's producers, Elite Racing. Those selected are hopeful that they'll be featured in local newspapers and on television. Upbeat music is favored—who wants to struggle running to a depressing song? Despite the rock and roll label, judges are looking for salsa, reggae, alternative, classic rock, and country music makers as well. Controversial lyrics or costumes are disallowed.

Spectators watch not just the race, but the entertainment, too. Bands are urged to play their best songs, which can be repeated often since the primary audience composed of runners changes by the minute. Spectators hearing the same song over and over tend to move on and visit more concerts along the race course.

Runners who compete in multiple Rock 'n' Roll events are eligible for the Heavy Medal Series, a kind of frequent flier award program for runners. Complete six Rock 'n' Roll marathons or half-marathons in one year (Elite Racing also produces the Country Music Marathon and the ING Philadelphia Distance Run, a half-marathon) and you'll receive a medal similar to the emblem on Superman's chest. Five and you are considered a "Rock Star" with a medal to match, even if all the races are half-marathons. Four full marathons and you receive a glittery gold "Rock" ornament that resembles a necklace that Diddy (aka Sean John Combs) would wear. Award jewelry can be had by running as few as two half-marathons if you like to chase medals. That's why organizers ask, "Got Bling?"

P.F. CHANG'S ROCK 'N' ROLL ARIZONA

LOCATION: PHOENIX - SCOTTSDALE - TEMPE, ARIZONA
MONTH: JANUARY
DISTANCE/AVERAGE FIELD: 26.2 MILES/8,000; 13.1 MILES/24,000

TELEPHONE: 800-311-1255
WEBSITE: www.rnraz.com

Arizona in January is tempting for a runner wanting to get away from the cold and celebrate Martin Luther King weekend out of town. With temperatures wavering between 50 and 70 degrees Fahrenheit (40 degrees Fahrenheit at the start) it's easy to warm up on the flat course that links three cities in greater Phoenix.

Southwest urban running includes many shopping centers and strip malls. Camelback Mountain and the Phoenix Mountain Range in the distance offer a bit of scenic respite. Far and away, the best distraction is from bands and cheerleading squads, quick to personalize their routines when they see you coming down the race course. It leaves you feeling like supportive friends and family are on the sidelines.

Participants have said that they'd like to see more gels and a better grade of energy drink on the course, but are fans of discount meal deals supplied by sponsor P.F. Chang's. The Chinese bistro chain restaurant is a popular spot for runners before and after the race.

ROCK 'N' ROLL HALF-MARATHON
LOCATION: VIRGINIA BEACH, VIRGINIA
MONTH: AUGUST/SEPTEMBER
DISTANCE/AVERAGE FIELD: 13.1 MILES/22,000

TELEPHONE: 800-311-1255
WEBSITE: www.rnrvb.com

Virginia Beach, a popular summer resort, hosts this half-marathon on Labor Day weekend with the race ending on the oceanfront boardwalk. Fourteen stages with bands on the course contribute to the party atmosphere. The post-race concert features name entertainment—Goo Goo Dolls and Counting Crows have played to packed beachside audiences.

Rock and roll, reggae, or blues—there's a new sound each mile inspiring runners with an element of surprise. It helps take your mind off the heat. Temperatures can reach 80 degrees Fahrenheit for the race, which has a 4-hour cut-off time. Don't expect ocean breezes to provide much relief in the crowded field. Falling on a holiday weekend, Rock 'n' Roll Half-Marathon has become so popular it sells out months in advance, despite a limit of 22,000 runners.

The race has the largest purse for a half-marathon in the United States. In 2008, more than $80,000 was awarded to top men and women finishers in several categories. Currently, the Verizon Wireless American Music Festival coincides with the race, featuring forty bands throughout the weekend and at the postrace concert.

ROCK 'N' ROLL MARATHON

LOCATION: SAN DIEGO, CALIFORNIA
MONTH: MAY/JUNE
DISTANCE/AVERAGE FIELD: 26.2 MILES/22,000

TELEPHONE: 800-311-1255
WEBSITE: www.rnrmarathon.com

It all started in San Diego, in 1998, with the first Rock 'n' Roll Marathon. Since then, combining live music and long-distance running is an undisputed success, as evidenced by an extension of the brand to other cities and many sold-out races. Twenty-six entertainment stages line this course and 1,500 cheerleaders are in store, in case you need encouragement to finish.

Appearing in the race's inaugural year and now a long-sought-out favorite is the Running Elvis pack. The collection of King of Rock and Roll wannabes sports black sideburns and wigs, often removed at water stops for a douse on the head to prevent overheating. Running-friendly Elvis costumes are now custom-made, available through the Rock 'n' Roll Marathon website. They come complete with non-chafing wicking material, pockets to hold energy gels, big collars, wide belts, and sequins in white Lycra® or turquoise print.

Elvises sing their hearts out, encouraging runners and spectators to belt out "Jailhouse Rock" or "Blue Suede Shoes." Known to commandeer music stages on the course, they'll also sing whatever the band is playing. The ring-toting romancers will get down on their knees and ask women to marry them, before running away.

By far, the biggest concern of the race is a 3-mile stretch of canted road on Highway 163 toward the end of mile 7. Runners have become so cramped that they're forced to stop running. Even those who originally thought the slant couldn't be that bad now welcome a course change. The nasty banked road has become a race legend.

Crowds made up of 22,000 runners and their well-wishing family and friends create car and pedestrian traffic woes. Participants have had difficulties getting to the start and walking for miles postrace to reach their car or public transportation.

The concert that night is a popular event. Headline entertainment has featured Seal, Hootie & the Blowfish, Chicago, and Huey Lewis & the News. One ticket is included with your race registration. You can buy tickets for additional guests.

Rock and roll goes hand in hand with partying, drawing runners who would rather linger on the course and delay crossing the finish. A 7-hour cutoff time applies and several timed checkpoints must be met during the race. Be wary of your official start time, not chip time, to meet these restrictions, and avoid too much distraction from all the entertainment on the course if you want to collect your medal.

ROCK 'N' ROLL SAN ANTONIO MARATHON & HALF-MARATHON

LOCATION: SAN ANTONIO, TEXAS

MONTH: NOVEMBER

DISTANCE/AVERAGE FIELD: 26.2 MILES/10,000, 13.1 MILES/20,000

TELEPHONE: 800-311-1255

WEBSITE: www.rnrsa.com

San Antonio sold out their inaugural year in 2008 for the Rock 'n' Roll race series. The marathon and half-marathon are held mid-November. Deep in the heart of Texas, the race course passes the Alamo, where 189 Texans died fending off Mexican soldiers in 1836, and other sights reflective of the history of Spain and Mexico.

San Pedro, the nation's second-oldest park, King William, the first historic district in the U.S., and San Antonio Missions National Historic Park, encompassing four Spanish Catholic missions built in the 1700s, add to attractions on the course.

As in other Rock 'n' Roll races, bands line the course every mile, but here Mexican music is mixed in and the cheering squads have a southern flair. November temperatures average 60 degrees Fahrenheit, so the race can be a bit on the warmer side. Cutoff times at checkpoints are required and are according to starting-gun time, not chip time. Since the race has a wave start, coordinate the time requirements on your running watch.

The Finish Line Fiesta celebrates with food and entertainment Mexican-style. Headline name bands are scheduled for the postrace concert at the Alamodome.

ROCK 'N' ROLL HALF-MARATHON SAN JOSE

LOCATION: SAN JOSE, CALIFORNIA
MONTH: OCTOBER
DISTANCE/AVERAGE FIELD: 13.1 MILES/15,000

TELEPHONE: 800-311-1255
WEBSITE: www.rnrsj.com

Up the California coastline from where Rock 'n' Roll races began, runners boogie to Rock 'n' Roll San Jose, a half-marathon in early October. The course has some gradual hills, and winds its way downtown, past City Hall and the San Jose State University. As in other races in the series, bands and cheerleaders line the course which, here, takes you past Japantown. It's one of the last three historical Japanese neighborhoods in the U.S. with many traditional restaurants, stores, and well-known karaoke bars. San Jose Municipal Rose Garden, home to almost 200 varieties of the fragrant flower, lies along the back side of the course, in case you want to stop and smell the roses after the race.

The finish line is near Plaza de Cesar Chavez, a park that's a tribute to the labor leader and civil-rights activist who fought for better working conditions in the 1960s. His birthday is currently a holiday in eight U.S. states, including California. Here, a large postrace festival takes place. At night, a concert at HP Pavilion attracts headline talent like the Grammy-award-winning group Ozomatli.

Some roads reopen to traffic toward the end of the race, so if you're a slow runner or walker you can encounter traffic metering, where runners are stopped to allow traffic to cross. The website details traffic closures, important information for a race that's grown to 15,000 participants. Access to the start and finish gets very crowded on race day, so it's best to arrive very early.

MORE ROCK 'N' ROLL?

You can run to rock 'n' roll year-round with two new events. Rock 'n' Roll Seattle is a marathon and half-marathon in June: www.rnrseattle.com. The Rock 'n' Roll Chicago Half-Marathon takes place in August: www.rnrchicago.com.

RUNNING WILD

Running long enough and strenuously working muscles, perfectly nourished with oxygen from heaving breaths, dissolves the need to physically fight exercise. An effortless exertion takes effect, a more natural state of physical activity reminiscent of animals running in the wild.

That could account for the attraction of races that feature running alongside antelope and other wild animals on an African game preserve, or competitions pitting runner against beast such as the Running of the Bulls.

The primal desire to run can partly be explained by scientists who have studied the importance of long-distance running in human survival and evolution. One study of early *Homo* specimens (from whom we evolved two million years ago), identified twenty-six physical traits directly related to running.

Our running-friendly anatomy includes a well-developed Achilles tendon, which stores and releases energy, yet isn't necessary for simple walking. Then there are the buns, or gluteus maximus muscles, which keep the body from falling over when leaning forward during a run. Additional advantages include minimal hair covering our bodies, breathing through the mouth, and the ability to sweat, all of which enable us to expel heat.

It's hypothesized that a body designed to travel long distances by foot improved our predecessors' hunt for food, reproduction, and basic chances of survival. It may be why we're able to summon the strength to master marathon mileage, and why at times running feels completely natural. Our ancestors' ability to forage for food by chasing and spearing wild beasts could be linked to the rush humans experience while running alongside animals, or at least on their turf.

Several races in this section allow competitors to run in an African game preserve. If racing in the home territory of lions and tigers and bears (oh my) may be a bit too risky for you, there are tamer ways to exercise your primal running desires. One international series of runs raises funds for gorillas, an endangered species, while requiring you to dress up as the primate, costume included in the registration fee.

However you choose to "run wild," these chapters will send you on some amazing adventures, or at least give you a good story to tell while you're warming up at the next starting line.

THE BIG FIVE MARATHON®
Running Wild

LOCATION: ENTABENI GAME RESERVE, SOUTH AFRICA

MONTH: JUNE

DISTANCE/AVERAGE FIELD: 26.2 MILES/50, 13.1 MILES/25

TELEPHONE: (Denmark) +45-36-98-00-00, (U.S.) 714-963-5281

WEBSITE: www.big-five-marathon.com

Elephants, rhinoceroses, buffalo, lions, and leopards roaming the African plains are known as the "big five" to safari guides. Hunters consider them the most prized big-game catch. Tourists regard them as the most sought-after sightings—unless, of course, you are running the Red Cross Big Five Marathon and Half-Marathon through Entabeni Private Game Reserve. Then, perhaps, zebras, impalas, giraffes, and other less ferocious animals may suit you just fine.

In this race, there are no barriers between you and the wildlife—not a fence, or a pen, or even a river to divert them. More danger lurks with hippopotamuses and crocodiles that also call this African savannah home. Armed park rangers in Land Rovers, on horseback, and even in helicopters, traverse the course to try and prevent any oncoming crises. In case of a serious accident the helicopter is ready to take you to a hospital. Despite assurances that fierce animals are kept at a safe distance, this isn't a race for the faint of heart.

Runners encounter wildlife early into the race. Zebra

can be seen running across the plains, their black-and-white-striped backs cutting through tall grass. Herds of impalas cross the race course, leaving a runner to render time less important than granting the horned beasts' right-of-way.

Both the marathon and the half-marathon set out from the Lakeside Lodge on the upper escarpment in the game preserve. The course passes the Entabeni Monolith and other unique sandstone formations before heading to the lower plateau. That's where runners circle around an area dubbed lion land—can you guess why?—before heading up the valley once again.

The hilly terrain is challenging and often changing, requiring foot placement on dirt road, stone, grass, and even close to 4 miles of deep, beachlike sand. One runner described it as "a beautiful hell." You can find yourself on an open plain or a hill path, even a steep zigzagging downhill that can take a half-hour to descend.

The biggest challenge is toward the end. Marathoners run down a ridge with a beautiful view of the plateau's lake, then climb a demanding 1,640 feet for almost 2 miles, on an uneven stone surface. It took one runner over 30 minutes to scale, resorting to walking backward and sideways to overcome his tired legs.

It's not unheard-of to cross paths with a rhino, see a giraffe, or find baboons playing near the course. An ostrich greeted one runner at the end of her race. Spectators at the finish line amount to approximately 30 locals. This may not sound like much of a cheering section, but what they lack in number they sure make up for in volume.

Everest Marathon: Winding your way around the Himalayan Mountains is like running in heaven. The starting line, at 17,007 feet, stands at the foot of the world's tallest mountain. *Credit: Alex Wood*

Credit: KP Communications, LLC

Antarctica Marathon: Runners scaling Collins Glacier are challenged not to slip and fall on the sheet of ice. *Credit: David McGonigal*

Pikes Peak Marathon® & Pikes Peak Ascent®: Above the tree line, runners attack the toughest ascent of the race to reach the summit of Pikes Peak, at 14,050 feet. Half-marathoners will have finished the competition, while marathoners reverse course and run down the boulder laden mountain.
Credit: Courtesy of Pikes Peak Marathon

Reggae Marathon: Jamaica's best chefs from well-known resorts prepare a gourmet pasta party that includes local fruits and seafood. Runners vote for their favorite dishes in the island-wide cooking competition.
Credit: Errol Anderson—Reggae Marathon

Draft Day 5K: A 50-yard line finish on the New York Giants Stadium football field is a thrill for both children and adults, even if you're not a sports fanatic. *Credit: KP Communications, LLC*

Great Wall of China Marathon: Climbing 60,000 steps, all shapes and sizes, with 1,000 years of history under your sneakers makes this one of my favorite races. Post-race massage on the Great Wall of China is an ideal way to wait for other runners to finish. *Credit: KP Communications, LLC*

Cigna Falmouth Road Race: Running a 7-mile course along the Cape Cod coast on a sunny day makes this an ideal summer race. Runners round historic Nobska Lighthouse, built in 1876. *Credit: Don Borowski*

Covered Bridges Half-Marathon: Taftsville Covered Bridge is one of many quaint New England landmarks on the route. Historic barns and general stores also enhance the scenery. *Credit: KP Communications, LLC*

Burro Days World Championship Pack Burro Race: Running with burros is an acquired skill not to be taken lightly. The Fairplay, Colorado, competition is the first event in the Triple Crown of Pack Burro Races. *Credit: Kathy Barr*

Ragnar Relay Northwest Passage: Mutiny on Whidbey Island, Washington, by one of the 300 teams competing in the 24-hour relay race that runs along the Pacific coastline. *Credit: Brian Nicholson*

Great Gorilla Run, London, England: Pack your own banana at this costume mandatory event in London. The charity race is a fundraiser to save endangered species. *Credit: Tariq Sheikh*

Big Sur International Marathon: The cliff-hugging course traces California's northern coastline. Listening to wildlife and waves pounding the surf have prompted runners to say that the race is a spiritual experience. *Credit: Bill Burleigh*

Great Ocean Road Marathon:
Twists and turns Down Under challenge runners on one of the world's most beautiful routes, located on Australia's southern coast. *Credit: Shane Goss/ licoricegallery.com*

Lantau Mountain Marathon:
The yellow course marker stamped K.O.T.H. (King of the Hills) deserves its title. The back half of the race course is on the ridge of the farthest mountain range. *Credit: KP Communications, LLC*

Intercontinental Istanbul Eurasia Marathon: Competitors crossing the Bosphorus Bridge run from Asia to Europe in the only marathon in the world that sets foot on two continents. *Credit: Merve Yilmaz*

Mount Kilimanjaro Marathon & Climb: A stretcher on the trail that leads to the summit of Africa's highest mountain shows just how primitive medical care can be on adventure marathon trips. *Credit: KP Communications, LLC*

Red Cross Big 5 Marathon®: Entebeni Game Reserve is the racecourse on this running safari. Start time depends on the proximity of the local pride of lions. *Credit: Adventure-Marathon.com*

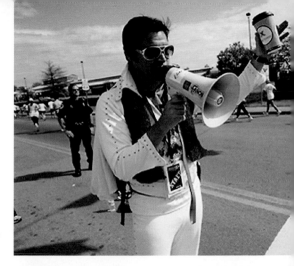

Country Music Marathon & ½ Marathon: Elvis sightings are part of the charm in this Nashville race.
Credit: Courtesy of the Country Music Marathon & ½ Marathon

Marathon du Médoc: The race can wait when wine tastings at Bordeaux's finest chateaux grace the marathon. Fresh-shucked oysters, grilled fillet, and cheese are also served to runners mid-race.
Credit: AMCM/DeTienda/Dubroca

Marabana Havana Marathon: In Cuba, competitors struggle in the 90 degree Fahrenheit heat and 85 percent humidity near Moro Castle, a fortress built in 1589. *Credit: KP Communications, LLC*

Inca Trail to Machu Picchu Marathon: "The Lost City of the Incas," hidden for 500 years, is the finish line for this endurance event. The course demands an altitude climb of 5,400 feet over three summits in the Andes Mountains, in Peru. *Credit: Carl Yarbrough*

Ragnar Relay Del Sol: Team members hand off the baton at sunset on the overnight relay race from Wickenburg to Scottsdale, Arizona. *Credit: Brian Nicholson*

Water stations every 3 miles are draped with tablecloths and are meticulously tended by waiters in uniform. For obvious reasons there are cutoff times, currently 6 hours for the marathon and 4 hours for the half-marathon. Who would want to stay out there with carnivorous nocturnal animals anyway?

Before race day, you can drive the course to see why you'll need to factor in a 25 to 75 percent slower-than-average time for your marathon. The route is exposed to direct sunlight, with temperatures hovering around 50 degrees Fahrenheit. (Nighttime temperatures can get much colder and dip below freezing.) The only toilet facilities are at the beginning and end of the race, so when nature calls you must relieve yourself naturally.

This area was dubbed "Waterberg" by early settlers because of the many lakes, swamps, waterfalls, and rivers in the area. In high season, December to February, brief storms create powerful downpours. They replenish streams and other water sources, causing the red stone dunes to glimmer in the sun.

The race, organized by a Denmark-based outfit, recruits mostly Danish runners comprising a field of fewer than 100 women and men for both races. Runners have found it well-organized. Profits donated to the South African Red Cross amounted to $20,000 U.S. in 2007.

If the idea of running in the wild suits you, you'll begin your adventure with a two-hour drive from Johannesburg to the Limpopo Province, home of the Entabeni Game Reserve. Accommodations are available in a lodge, or you can opt for a luxury campsite. Tents at Wildside Camp come complete with beds, electricity, a private bath, and electric blankets. Campfires draw the guests out for nightcaps and to trade race stories. You are escorted back to your tent after dark because it's not uncommon for lions to visit the campsite. (Mornings, look for paw prints outside your sleeping quarters.) Prior to the race there are daily safari drives. You can admire the beauty of the animals and get familiar with the primal company that you'll encounter on the race course.

LIKE SAFARI RUNS?

The Victoria Falls Marathon and Half-Marathon are scenic safari races held in August. National Park guards monitor a route along the largest waterfall in the world. If you're up for traveling to Zimbabwe, with a border crossing to Zambia during the race, go to www.vicfallsmarathon.com.

BURRO DAYS "WORLD CHAMPIONSHIP" PACK BURRO RACE
Hauling Ass

LOCATION: FAIRPLAY, COLORADO

MONTH: JULY

DISTANCE/AVERAGE FIELD: 29 MILES/10 RUNNER-BURRO TEAMS, 15 MILES/15 RUNNER-BURRO TEAMS

TELEPHONE: 719-836-2659

WEBSITE: www.burrodays.com

Fairplay, Colorado, will never forget the burro's role in gold mining in this town, so not only is a marathon held in its honor, the four-legged beast gets to come along. The race takes place during Burro Days, a celebration of the gold rush, the last weekend in July. This 29-mile race, run over Mosquito Pass at an altitude of 13,179 feet in the rugged Rocky Mountains, requires each runner to lead a haltered burro by a rope no less than 15 feet long.

There are mishaps inherent in racing burros. Although donkeys have a reputation for stubbornness when you want them to move, their behavior proves differently in a race. The runner often trails the burro, which won't stop if the runner falls. The foremost threat is being dragged along the ground, near the trampling hooves of your running partner. Sexual politics can also prove a problem—between burros. One year, a winning team overcame their opponent when the female burro ahead was in heat and the male burro took off in pursuit. Then there are those asses that decide to lie down before crossing the finish line—a fleeting thought that tempts many marathon runners. It's understandable, though. It's hard work making it up a steep, off-road pass littered with boulders, fallen trees, and even deep snow.

Burros, the Spanish word for donkeys, must dress the part they played in gold-mining days. They're outfitted with a regulation pack saddle and prospecting gear including a pick, shovel, and gold pan. The equipment must meet a regulation minimum weight of 33 pounds. The runner's water, food, and clothing may be carried by the animal (just think, no need for baggage check), but can't be counted as part of the pack weight and the burro can never, ever carry you. Weigh-ins are mandatory before the start and at the finish. Any lost items from the gold-prospecting kit result in disqualification.

Like any good team, burro and runner train for the race. Subtle cues from the animal and developed techniques assist humans in coercing their critter through the course. Some tricks include pushing the donkey's behind and pulling the rope. It's a talent, to be sure: part animal husbandry, part running. The need for donkey diplomatic relations is evident when runners train solo on the course. They cut their finishing time in half when they leave their burro at home.

Veterans say getting to know your partner is critical, suggesting long overnight pack trips to enhance bonding before the race. What you feed and how you shoe your burro during the marathon can be as critical as your own nutrition and footwear.

Don't have a running partner? You can borrow a burro, but many runners have their own; some are even adopted from burro-rescue organizations. The race requires medical checkups at both ends of the race, where veterinarians check for drugs, injury, or mistreatment.

Some allowances that are perfectly acceptable in more traditional marathons are against the rules here. Pacing is a no-no for both runners and burros, as is trying to scare an opponent's running buddy.

Runner and burro must cross the finish line as a team,

but the animal's nose determines the winning time, whether or not the runner is behind the burro. A little prize money is available to winners and early finishers, but the race organization's slogan is "No ribbons, no wimps, no age groups," so don't expect a medal.

Spectators are not your usual sort. Don't take the shouting and profane slogans such as "Get your ass up the pass" personally. Organizers ask competitors to grin and bear the paying customers, who spend the day at gold-panning demonstrations, shooting galleries, barbecues, and other mining activities that were popular in the 1850s.

Finishing the 29-mile race course in less than 5 hours puts you among the best times. A shorter 15-mile race is also held. Women take top spots along with the men in many of these races. Crowds of 10,000 people are drawn to the event, as well as to the short-distance llama and dog races, parades, and cowboy church services featuring guitar playing and storytelling.

The Burro Days race is the first in a Triple Crown series of Colorado pack burro racing, held every year by the Western Pack Burro Ass-ociation. The shorter distance second and third races are in Leadville and Buena Vista respectively. Additional pack burro races are held throughout the state.

Legend has it that racing donkeys originated in mining days. Prospectors heading from a dig site to stake their claim raced one another to the mining office to protect their find. Actually, the event began in 1949 to attract tourists to celebrations commemorating gold-mining days. Still, there is a movement on for pack burro racing to be named Colorado's official state sport—the only competitive sport indigenous to Colorado.

LIKE BURRO RUNNING BUDDIES?

The Western Pack Burro Ass-ociation has a series of races in Colorado. Check them out at www.packburroracing .com.

Gorilla Runs
GO APE

You don't have to ask if there are bananas at these aid stations. You do have to dress up as a gorilla—not just the head, but a full-length costume—to compete in these events. They're held to raise money to prevent the extinction of the mountain gorilla.

If you've never run in a costume before, hitting a stride with the extra weight of a full-body suit covered with synthetic fur is a challenge. Considerable chafing will have you pining for your running shorts. How do you breathe comfortably? Believe me, ventilation is an issue! It's also tricky drinking water. Make sure your outfit has an adequate way of allowing you to hydrate—you may want to bring a straw. A strand of faux fur is often found in the water cups at aid stations.

Gorillas don't normally contend with these problems. They rarely drink because they get enough water from their diets. After suiting up, you just might want to kick back, relax, and save vying for a personal record for another day.

Running incognito certainly livens up the starting line,

providing an easy way to start a conversation with your fellow primates. For example, "Did you know that 'gorilla' is derived from the Greek word *Gorillai,* meaning a tribe of hairy women?" Although that may not be the best opening line, it's all for a good cause. And if you start to mysteriously crave leaves, shoots, and stems, not to worry, they are 86 percent of the herbivore's diet. Bananas aren't a major staple in a gorilla's diet. The fruit only makes up 1 percent of their meals. Bananas are in short supply in the forest, but there are plenty of them on the race course.

DENVER GORILLA RUN

LOCATION: DENVER, COLORADO
MONTH: OCTOBER
DISTANCE/AVERAGE FIELD: 3.5 MILES/1,000

TELEPHONE: 866-GORILLA (467-4552)
WEBSITE: www.denvergorillarun.com

The weekend before Halloween, the Gorilla Run in Denver is held by the Mountain Gorilla Conservation Fund, an international nonprofit, working toward saving the last remaining primates. Gorilla outfits are provided to participants who are informally grouped into divisions according to packs found in the wild: Amahoro, Mubare, Sabinyo, or Rushegura. Any similarity to the wild kingdom ends there, as Rollerblading, skateboarding, dog-walking, and baby-stroller-pushing gorillas lope through the mile-high city streets. Cyclists dressed as big bananas lead the way, eventually routing you to a bike path.

Gorilla-costume variations continue to be clever, slid over the mandatory gorilla outfit provided at on-site race registration, in select city locations, or, if you're out of state, by U.S. mail. Many are not what you'd associate with the primate. A beer can, toilet bowl, and juggler throwing clubs in the air for the duration of the race have been sighted. The race director presides over a costume contest dressed as a jailed poacher. One gorilla carried a woman over his shoulder. Who said chivalry King Kong–style was dead? A 2-story inflatable ape guides you to the start/finish line, in case you get lost in the urban jungle.

The required gorilla suit can make it cumbersome to run, and see (if you're wearing glasses), and breathe (if you're not used to the mile-high altitude). The suit limits peripheral vision, so be wary of gorillas on wheels whizzing past you, or fast primates whooshing by, like the pack that covered the 3.5-mile course in less than 15 minutes.

Gorilla suits don't have much of a mouthpiece, making drinking water more difficult than usual at the aid stations at 1-mile intervals. A lack of openings for the ears renders iPods impractical. Race officials suggest that you cut out the eyes, make a bigger nose and mouth, and leave the velcro vent in the back of the costume open for more air circulation. Scissors are provided at registration on race day to facilitate wardrobe adjustments. One year on a hot day, fifteen gorillas spontaneously jumped in the Platte River to cool off.

Prizes are awarded for the best costume. To be eligible you'll have to wear it throughout the race. There is a registration fee and suggested fund-raising component. Contributions go toward the Mountain Gorilla Conservation Fund, a nonprofit working with Rwandan and Ugandan governments to help causes for mountain gorillas and local residents. Efforts include building a veterinary school to train professionals to staff National Parks throughout Africa.

THE GREAT GORILLA RUN
LOCATION: **LONDON, ENGLAND**
MONTH: **SEPTEMBER**
DISTANCE/AVERAGE FIELD: **4.3 MILES/1,000**

TELEPHONE: (England) 020-7916-4974
WEBSITE: www.greatgorillas.org

British runners are keen on costumes at England's Great Gorilla Run, where you'll be surrounded by a multitude of competitors creatively expressing their inner gorilla. There are apes dressed in tennis whites holding a racquet, and leather vest and neckerchief-clad models donning cowboy hats. A *Baywatch*-style Pamela Anderson primate has graced the course, as well as a grass-skirted beast on a unicycle. Then of course there are more basic species simply toting large yellow inflatable bananas.

Don't have the required gorilla suit? Not to worry. It's provided in your registration kit, and yours to take home after the race. If you've saved your costume from the previous year, your registration fee will be reduced. The fund-raising component of this event is truly a commitment; you're required to raise 400 British pounds.

The primates are routed through metropolitan London, crossing the Thames several times, first at Tower Bridge, later at London Bridge, before passing the Tate Modern Museum and Saint Paul's Cathedral. Running gorillas have a lot of fun comparing costumes, getting photographed with tourists, and trying to convince casual joggers to join the pack. Don't disobey the course marshals. They are armed with giant yellow inflatable bananas and will strike when necessary. There's even a medal for race finishers because, come on, running in a full-length gorilla costume? It's hot in there.

The London Gorilla Run is held in September, when the weather can still be warm. If the sun comes out, runners get overheated and itchy in their full-length acrylic faux fur, and are tempted to take their heads off. (Now you can empathize with your dog, if you run with it during the summer.) Runners have had to enlarge the eyeholes so they can see better, and there's a lot of unintentional bumping on the course.

British television celebrities like Bill Oddie, a television writer and performer on the BBC conservation and wildlife shows, make an appearance. The London-based charity Gorilla Organization runs the event to raise money to protect the critically endangered species. There are only 723 known mountain gorillas left in the wilds of the Congo, Rwanda, and Uganda. Their numbers have grown by 20 percent since a charity was established by Dian Fossey, the well-known primatologist murdered while studying gorillas and protecting them from poachers and other dangers. Part of this organization's goal is to establish better living conditions and income from sources other than poaching, for locals sharing the primate habitat in the Congo.

The Great Gorilla Run is hoping to expand to other international and domestic cities. Links to new races can be accessed through the website.

NEW YORK ROAD RUNNERS EMPIRE STATE BUILDING RUN-UP
King Kong Revisted

LOCATION: NEW YORK, NEW YORK

MONTH: FEBRUARY

DISTANCE/AVERAGE FIELD: 86 FLIGHTS OF STAIRS; 1,576 STEPS/200

TELEPHONE: 212-736-3100

WEBSITE: www.esbnyc.com/tourism/tourism_specialevents_runup.cfm

---

"You owe me five dollars," chimed the man on the phone next to me. He had made a bet with his friend that he could run to the top of the tallest building in New York City. He stood next to a guy in a gorilla suit, as competitors put on dry clothes at baggage claim, after the New York Road Runners (NYRR) Empire State Building Run-Up.

Although the original movie starring Fay Wray and the remake with Jessica Lange seem dated, who can forget the super-steroid-sized, 3-story-high gorilla climbing the needle-nosed skyscraper for the woman he loved? It's enough to make you want to scale 86 stories.

Climbing the 1,576 stairs to the Observation Deck, almost a quarter mile above Manhattan, requires some of the same endurance found in running. Despite my marathon training, I was so out of breath lifting my entire weight step after step that I had to stop often during this unusual race. Hopeful applicants are asked to fill out a form detailing their physical experience, so competitors can be carefully selected. One qualification posted by New York Road Runners judges reserves "the right to accept or reject entries, as necessary, to accommodate the narrowness of the stairwell" at 40 inches wide.

Those lucky enough to wear a running number cross the starting line in the art deco marble lobby, and are quickly funneled through the fire stairs door. A human swell of legs and arms, in tank tops and running shorts, squeeze through a door frame designed for two people. There's not much relief provided by a multiple-wave start—two for men, one for women, reflecting the three-to-one male-to-female ratio.

Past the first hurdle, competitors "take the hill," racing up stairs. It quickly becomes clear that the energy required isn't parallel to running. Better off are those who trained by running stadiums instead of stair machines that don't require each leg to bear your full weight. Many competitors' optimistic techniques of two steps up at a time and fast paces are adjusted downward, causing the crowd in the stairwell to quickly spread out. Survival techniques kick in; hanging on to the handrail serves to avoid inevitable trips—

when tired legs don't lift quite high enough—and to help swing you around landings.

Office workers play the role of spectators, standing in stairwells cheering on competitors, sometimes offering cups of water. It's a welcome gesture, since there are no aid stations until after the finish. Although it's the middle of winter, the building is heated, so select a running outfit accordingly. Despite the interior warmth, there are those who still opt for covering their head with a blond Fay Wray/Jessica Lange wig, or suit up head to toe in gorilla garb.

Flight after flight, the motion is repetitive. Clearing the 8-inch-high stairs becomes more challenging with every floor. The gray-painted interior seems endless, despite the race technically measuring only .2 miles. Counting off floors keeps you mentally occupied—you can understand why King Kong scaled the building's more scenic exterior.

Runners reaching the enclosed observatory on the 86th floor are led to the outdoor promenade. A short stretch on the outside deck, underneath the Empire State Building's famous pinnacle, brings you to the finish.

It's rewarding to have New York City at your feet after climbing your way to the top. On a bright, sunny day you can see 80 miles in every direction, across New York, New Jersey, Pennsylvania, Connecticut, and Massachusetts.

It takes much less time to climb the 1,050 feet to the top of the world's tenth-tallest building, than it feels. The average finish time is 17 minutes and the current record is 9:33. This is one race where your official race photo may mean more than most, but not before purchasing a stuffed gorilla at the concession stand.

LIKE CLIMBING?

If the NYRR Empire State Building Run-Up whets your appetite, then check out www.towerrunning.com. Mountain runner Michael Reichetzeder has compiled an international list of stair races. It includes one on the world's longest staircases, at 11,674 steps along a Swiss Alp funicular. There's also a race that mimics climbing the height of Mount Everest at 29,029 feet, after completing 100 roundtrip staircase climbs in Radebeul, Germany. There are many more stair races to run, in more than fifteen U.S. cities, including San Francisco, Chicago, and Miami.

SPIRITUAL EXPERIENCES

Running is an exercise removed from life's trappings. Few material items are required to set out on a run, and attaining it is a simple, uncomplicated routine right outside your front door.

After overcoming the resistance inherent in a warm-up, slipping into a consistent pace can be mesmerizing. Deep breaths required to maintain a rhythmic speed nourish both body and soul. It's not uncommon to find yourself drifting to another level where you can unlock life's complexities. Once in your groove, there's an incredible peace of mind, far from a world buzzing with demands.

With this perfect rhythm calming your soul, there are instances of a deep appreciation of a sunrise, a forest, and other gifts from Mother Nature. So strong is its power that runners say they've felt close to God, or to a loved one who has passed away.

These feelings aren't derived from one known formula or running technique. But there are similarities that runners describe to reach this unique place. Being surrounded by magnificent beauty helps, or in a place where generations have gathered to practice their religion or honor their spiritual leader.

Incredible races at unique locales within this chapter are conducive to an incredible sense of peace. Surrounded by the world's tallest mountains in the Himalayas at the Everest Marathon, I felt like I was running in heaven. A cathedral of redwood trees alongside the dramatic cliff-hugging course at Big Sur International Marathon conjure thoughts and feelings that transcend running times. These runs may inspire you to travel far, or give you comfort simply by knowing that others share the same peace of mind that you've achieved by running in beautiful places.

BIG SUR INTERNATIONAL MARATHON
California's Most Beautiful Coastline

LOCATION: BIG SUR, CALIFORNIA

MONTH: APRIL

DISTANCE/AVERAGE FIELD: 26.2 MILES/4,500; 21 MILES/1,000; 10.6 MILES/1,600; 9 MILES/1,000; 3.1 MILES/1,200

TELEPHONE: 831-625-6226

WEBSITE: www.bsim.org

Pacific Coast Highway, hugging the cliff-laden California shore 85 miles south of San Francisco, is one of the most beautiful drives in America. In 1986, County Judge Bill Burleigh was driving to his cabin and saw a sign that said BIG SUR, 26 MILES. A runner, and an influential local, Burleigh obtained a permit to close the road, attracted 1,800 competitors, and the Big Sur International Marathon was born.

Often described as a religious experience, the race begins by redwood trees more than 200 feet high and 10 feet in diameter in Pfeiffer Big Sur State Park. They tower over runners in the early-morning mist, the scent of fresh forest filling the air. Twenty white doves grace the starting line, ready for release in tandem with thousands of legs scrambling to begin. Nervous chatter common before a race gives way to the pure sound of sneakers rhythmically pounding the race course. The way the sun pierces the forest canopy for a 5-mile stretch is reminiscent of light beaming through stained-glass windows. Many who have experienced it describe this race as a journey instead of a marathon.

Runners leaving the forest are greeted by ocean cliffs and rolling hills, following the race course on Highway One. Some participants may be fortunate to sight whales migrating, hear sea lions on shore, and glimpse flocks of birds stretching their wings across an endless sky. Mother Nature is at her finest.

The closed road prevents access to all but the runners. The uncharacteristic quiet, combined with waves steadily pounding the cliffs, provides runners a setting to let their thoughts go.

"I ran with my mom for 10 miles and she's been dead for 10 years," said one competitor.

Runners at Big Sur form unique bonds, since words of encouragement come from one another instead of the usual cheers and applause from the sidelines. Expansive ranches line one side of the road. Thousands of cows graze the rolling hills. The next 5 miles are flat, relatively speaking, until Hurricane Point, marking the start of a 2-mile climb. Named for the wind whipping the top of the hill, it's the highest elevation at 560 feet, but runners are still less than halfway through the race. That milestone is saved for Bixby Bridge.

Bixby Bridge, an impressive arch structure featured in many car commercials, spans 714 feet over rocky shoreline and turbulent waters from Bixby Creek, flowing into the ocean. Approaching it on a downhill for 1 mile, don't think that you're hallucinating if you hear music. At the bridge's end sits a Yamaha grand piano. If the wind is right, you can hear classical music a mile away.

How can you get a grand piano placed on the Pacific Coast Highway? Courtesy of Yamaha in San Francisco, it arrives by flatbed truck, fully insured by race organizers. Jonathan Lee serenaded runners with his original music for over 16 years; now you'll identify his scores with having completed the first half of one of the most beautiful races in the world. Lee's CD sells at the race registration expo for those who plan to recount the moment. Currently a local pianist is selected to play the ivories, continuing the musical tradition.

As the course veers inland toward Carmel at mile 21, expensive homes surround the route to Point Lobos, a marine reserve and whaling site at the turn of the twentieth century. Described as one of the greatest meetings of land and water in the world, a sharp drop just off the coast that's more characteristic of a mid-ocean location, it attracts unusual underwater animal and plant life, including 2,000-year-old wind-sculpted cypress trees.

Once past the reserve you can see Pebble Beach Golf Course and Carmel Beach, one of the nicest beaches in California. Signs designed to distract runners from aching feet and sore muscles are planted every so often along the course. One urges participants to LOOK BACK before entering town and leaving the magnificent coastline scenery behind.

The grandeur of all this rolling countryside comes at a price, including hills, wind, and canted road. It's a challenging race course that has earned Big Sur International Marathon billing as one of the toughest marathons in the United States. The website includes tips for mastering the hills and sells a book on training for the event. Water stops are plentiful at every 2 miles, with an extra one right before the finish at mile 25.

From the 5-mile mark, outside the redwood forest, the 21-mile race follows the same route as the marathon. It's the first distance to sell out, attracting walkers who are 90 percent of the field, and also required to return within the 6½-hour cutoff time. The 10.6-miler starts much closer to the marathon finish, and is also quite popular. A 9-miler and 5K (3.1 miles) start at the marathon finish and run a loop, heading south.

In November, Big Sur sponsors a half-marathon on a different course in downtown Monterey Bay, about 3 miles north of Carmel. November entrants may also register for a 10-mile walk and 5K.

The sign that inspired Judge Burleigh to organize the race is actually for Big Sur Village. You'll find it at the mouth of the Carmel Valley, at the intersection of Rio Road and Highway One. Several years ago someone hand-painted a marathon distance correction, so the sign reads BIG SUR, 26.2 MILES.

LIKE REDWOOD TREES?

If running under redwood trees—the world's tallest living things—brings you peace of mind, check out the Avenue of the Giants Marathon, Half-Marathon, & 10K, in May, in Humboldt Redwoods State Park in northern California: www.theave.org. The course scenery is also breathtaking at the Humboldt Redwoods Marathon, Half-Marathon, & 5K, in October: www.RedwoodsMarathon.org.

EVEREST MARATHON
The Highest Marathon in the World

LOCATION: GORAK SHEP, NEPAL
(690 feet below Mount Everest Base Camp)
MONTH: NOVEMBER/DECEMBER
DISTANCE/AVERAGE FIELD: 26.2 MILES/75

TELEPHONE: (United Kingdom) +44-1539-445-445
WEBSITE: www.everestmarathon.org.uk

The dark, jagged summit of the world's highest mountain soars so high, it touches the jet stream, creating a trail of white ice crystals that contrasts with the blue sky. Mount Everest dares you not to pay homage to it as you run in the shadow of lesser snowcapped peaks, formidable in their own right. Sheer height from mountains surrounding you in every direction helps you understand why locals consider the mountains gods. You're so high up that you can hear silence. It's like no other place on earth. Running the Everest Marathon is like running in heaven.

Getting to the race start is a journey in itself. The 2-week excursion begins in Lukla, at 11,318 feet. Your prop plane lands on an uncomfortably short runway pointing straight into the mountainside, prompting prayers for a competent pilot and no technical difficulties. After two nights acclimatizing in Namche Bazaar, you hike to Gorak Shep at 17,007 feet.

Tracing the race course backward on your trek, you're at altitudes most people will never experience in their lifetime. Mastering switchbacks that rise and fall 500 feet, you begin to understand why the Everest Marathon has been called the toughest marathon in the world. The Gorak Shep race start is just 690 feet below Everest Base Camp, where climbers anxious to conquer the world's highest mountain embark and almost 200 have never returned. You quickly learn to pay homage to Sagarmatha, the Nepali name for Everest meaning "Goddess of the Sky."

A simple blue banner announcing EVEREST MARATHON RACE START is hung on a lone teahouse, a simple structure resembling a woodshed. Before you take your mark, plan to double your average marathon time. Your metabolism will struggle to harvest enough oxygen from the thin air to keep your body functioning, let alone meet the demands of a 26.2-mile race on switchbacks. This literally means you can be running all day if your average marathon time is over 3 hours.

Pray for clear skies because there are no up-to-the-minute weather reports. My year, snow delayed the race for almost an hour while officials tried to determine the severity of the storm. As a precaution, I ran the first half of the marathon in hiking boots. Getting stranded in a whiteout on a course in the Himalayan Mountains can be fatal since the unmarked course requires running on ledges carved into mountainsides, climbing boulders, and following a dirt trail that's easily camouflaged when covered in snow. There were no communications among race officials along the course. Luckily, the storm tapered off to reveal heavenly surroundings.

Teahouses, where basic medical assistance, cookies, and

water were available, dot the course about every 3 miles. Still, the route feels quite isolated and participants are required to run the entire 26.2 miles with a backpack stuffed with emergency gear. This includes waterproofs, a bivvy bag (a plastic shell that provides warmth), flashlight and extra batteries, long underwear, hat, mittens, and a whistle. Unlike most other marathons, it's mandatory for runners to look out for one another, whether or not coming to someone's aid delays your time. This may mean interrupting your race to assist or redirect someone who has veered off-course. Ignore this rule and you will be disqualified.

Acclimatizing is essential. We trekked for 3 weeks to the starting line. Currently, political unrest in Nepal means runners start farther up the trail, by flying into Lukla and trekking for a little over two weeks to the race start.

Physically, no other race has demanded more from my body. Tears streamed down my face closing in on the end of the race. Then, 50 yards from the finish, a line of yaks crossed my path. I waited for the 2,400-pound long-haired bovines to pass. Their sharp 3-foot horns were more threatening than adding a few minutes to my time.

Just in case, insurance coverage is required for both the trek to the start and the race itself, including emergency helicopter evacuation, medical expenses, and returning an injured runner to his or her homeland. Recommended insurers are provided by the race organizer.

Pack light because a 26-pound-per-person weight limit is required for your duffel bag, balanced three at a time on Sherpas' backs and banded across their foreheads. They manage this feat walking in rubber flip-flops, or even bare-foot, scaling the same steep, cliff-hugging switchbacks as we did. Minimalist packing includes your sleeping bag, thermal mat, down jacket, and other gear for temperatures that dip below freezing at night. Add toiletries and personal items, and not much more than one change of clothes can be accommodated. But don't forget a bag of quality chocolate from home, essential for giving you a lift during those all-day treks.

High-altitude camping equipment, such as a water purifier and lithium batteries, which keep charged longer in cold weather, are essential. The list of necessities is included with race registration information on the website. I spent ample time researching the most appropriate brands for my trip and finding stores that had very knowledgeable salespeople, sometimes having hour-long conversations about the advantage of one breathable fabric over another. It was a great education, well worth the time, and there was more than one occasion on a subfreezing night when I was thankful that I did my homework.

Sleeping quarters are two-person tents, so hopefully you're paired with someone you like. Breakfast and dinner are ladled out on reusable metal plates and cups, served on the food tent's long communal table. Lunches are more informal, if that's possible, served outside mid-trek on a waterproof tarp, with views rivaling any classy restaurant. During the daylong treks you'll be happy to stop for a Snickers bar, Coke, and a slim selection of other treats at village tea-houses along the trail.

Meals consist mostly of rice, beans, and dal bhat, a soup

of spiced lentils and rice. We were served tasteless custard for dessert. Between the bland, low-fat cuisine and a common high altitude side effect of appetite loss, most people shed pounds over and above those generally lost in marathon training.

Daily bathing is an unnecessary luxury up here. The best place to freshen up is the Dudh Kosi River, sourced from glacial runoff and melting snow. Sponge baths make the frigid water more tolerable. Still, it's undeniably refreshing once you get used to it. At this altitude air pollution is seriously reduced, so daily cleansing isn't essential.

Postrace, a hot shower of a rustic variety can be purchased for a few dollars at teahouses. Boiling water from a pot heated on a wooden fire is poured into a container with a spigot flowing down to a cold, cement basement or an outdoor cabin. Carefully negotiating the pull handle allows you brief interludes of scalding water. If you want to break ranks, there is a luxury hotel with hot showers and sit-down toilets an hour's climb from the finish line at Namche Bazaar, but after the marathon you may not feel like a hike.

Entries for the Everest Marathon, held every other year, are restricted. Race director Diana Penny Sherpani selects applicants based on athletic experience and previous marathon times. Her policy is first-come, first-served and the race usually sells out. One companion per runner is allowed, although my year there weren't many. Sherpani needs 10 to 12 nonrunners to work as race-day volunteers. Depending on how many people are bringing a significant other, you may get special consideration if you're accompanied by someone who is willing to help.

More than a handful of Nepalese enter the race despite being part of a culture that considers running a curious pastime. Don't underestimate the locals; they are used to the altitude and have dominated the top finishing times for years without any sophisticated running gear. It's not unheard-of for someone to run the entire 26.2 miles in flip-flops.

Participants must pass a medical exam two days before the race to screen for altitude sickness. I saw two men denied entry after spending several thousand dollars on the trip, taking a month off work, and trekking for 3 weeks, not to mention countless hours spent marathon training. Trusting the medical team's decision is essential. Emergency facilities that could make a life-or-death difference are hours away only if you're lucky enough to access a helicopter and have good weather, otherwise figure on weeks to reach aid.

Loved ones who crave the great outdoors won't be disappointed if they come with you, even if they're not runners. Not many people have the privilege of seeing the world's highest mountain.

You'll meet many British runners on this trip since the organizer is based in England. One of their race customs, raising money for charity, is required of all participants. Donations go to the Everest Marathon Fund, supporting medical and educational needs in rural Nepal. During the Everest Marathon's 12-year tenure, almost one million dollars has been raised.

Shedding most of your worldly goods and learning how little you really need to survive is eye-opening. Living in the

Himalayas, surrounded by breathtaking mountains by day and blankets of stars at night, more plentiful and brighter than you've ever seen, and Mother Nature makes an unforgettable impression. Focusing purely on survival in extreme conditions gave me a new perspective. The experiences to be had at the Everest Marathon are life-changing.

LIKE THE HIMALAYAN MOUNTAINS?

If you are shut out of the Everest Marathon or want to compete in a year when it's not being held, the Tenzing-Hillary Marathon has more recently been created: www.everestmarathon.com. The trek to the starting line retraces the steps of Sir Edmund Hillary and his famous guide, Tenzing Norgay Sherpa, before they began their historic summit. The course is mostly similar to the Everest Marathon, but starts at a slightly higher elevation at 17,572 feet, at the base camp where Everest summit attempts begin.

GREAT OCEAN ROAD INTERNATIONAL MARATHON

Down Under Wonder

LOCATION: LORNE, AUSTRALIA

MONTH: MAY

DISTANCE/AVERAGE FIELD: 28 MILES/350, 14.3 MILES/900, 8.7 MILES/600, 4 MILES/300

TELEPHONE: (Australia) +61-03-5224-2466

WEBSITE: www.greatoceanroadmarathon.com.au

One of the most beautiful roads in the world is the race course for the Great Ocean Road International Marathon and Half-Marathon. The two-lane highway is mostly covered by trees and vegetation reminiscent of sketches drawn in books for children's fairy tales. Winding its way around the curves and cliffs, the road traces Australia's southern coastline. Looking out into the Indian Ocean, the island of Tasmania is the only land standing between you and Antarctica.

The race measures 1.75 miles longer than your average marathon. It sets off from Lorne, a small town rich in history and lined with seaside cafés, restaurants, and shops. Its 1870s-era post office marks the starting line on the Great Ocean Road, 86 miles southwest of Melbourne. The half-marathon, 1.2 miles longer than average, begins midcourse by the Kennett River. Races of shorter distances—the Paradise Valley 14K (8.7 miles) and Marriners Lookout 6.5K (4 miles)—are offered on Saturday, the day before the longer-distance races. They start and finish at the Apollo Bay Hotel.

Great Ocean Road is closed from Lorne to Apollo Bay for the event, so you don't have to worry about cars veering around cliff-hugging roads or the smell of exhaust. But road closures also reduce the amount of spectators on the course, save for small towns where the locals come out to encourage you.

The elevation is a challenge, rising from sea level to as high as 236 feet, once in the first half of the marathon, and twice, mercilessly, on the second half of the course. Rolling hills scattered throughout the race add to your hardship, making personal bests almost impossible. Count on the magnificent scenery to help alleviate your pain.

The course weaves around rugged coastal terrain with mighty waves pounding against jagged cliffs. Ocean spray carried by the wind lightly showers runners on the road above. A stretch of eucalyptus trees—the Australian koala's natural habitat—lines the roadway. One runner who was fortunate to spot the cute, furry creature said it's almost enough to make you forget that your knees are killing you.

Despite its beauty, Ocean Road International Marathon owns a small field and corresponding budget. Race numbers are written with black felt-tip marker by volunteers. Several runners reported that aid tables are sparse, devoid of gels or sports drinks, so bring your own energy essentials. The cutoff time for the marathon is 6¹/₂ hours, while runners need to finish the 23K race in 4 hours.

The winter weather can be temperamental because the seasons are reversed in the Southern Hemisphere. Temperatures range from a sunny, warm 70 degrees Fahrenheit to 40 degrees Fahrenheit with cold and icy rain. In 2007, the night before the race, gale-force winds tore off roof tiles, although by the next morning the storm had blown over. Runners have had to compete in wind and rain. Be prepared with a wide range of running gear. Don't forget to bring sunblock, as most of the course is exposed to the rays.

Both races end at the Apollo Bay Hotel, in a slightly larger town than at the race start. Not much farther down the road are the Twelve Apostles, an impressive collection of water-carved limestone formations towering next to the coast in Port Campbell National Park. It's worth driving there when you're rested after the race.

Great Ocean Road International Marathon held its inaugural race in 2005. Given the scenery and outdoor adventure activities available in the area, the field for this young race undoubtedly will increase in the years to come.

INCA TRAIL TO MACHU PICCHU
Above the Clouds

LOCATION: INCA TRAIL, CUSCO, PERU
MONTH: MAY/JUNE/AUGUST
DISTANCE/AVERAGE FIELD: 27.5 MILES/50

TELEPHONE: 800-289-9470
WEBSITE: www.andesadventures.com

Machu Picchu was inhabited by the Incas, South American Indians who ruled the region more than 600 years ago. Abandoned in the 1500s, the city was rediscovered by an American historian in 1911, although it's still shrouded in mystery. Theories on its purpose range from an emperor's estate to a spiritual center where the mountains aligned with astronomical events. Whatever the intention, it's a magical place and the Inca Trail to Machu Picchu Marathon takes you there, on the ancient stone road leading to "The Lost City."

Runners begin their journey in Cusco, once the capital of the Incan empire, perched 11,150 feet high in the Andes

Mountains. The race is designed as a package trip and there is not much time to acclimate. That might convince you to arrive several days earlier if you're not used to running at altitude. Currently, 3 days of 4- to 8-mile runs before the marathon are scheduled at villages and campsites at elevations ranging from 8,400 to 12,350 feet.

The stretch of trail to Machu Picchu runs close to Llactapata, an archeological site filled with temples and terrace farms. After a night of camping, it's here that the marathon begins before dawn on one of South America's most popular hiking trails. The 4-day ascent for hikers must be completed by runners in one day for a race that's 1.3 miles longer than a regulation 26.2 marathon. Add the three-summit climb to get to Machu Picchu, an ascent of almost a mile, and this may be the most demanding race you'll ever run.

The Inca Trail is primarily a stone-laid path cutting into cliffs with many uneven steps that can measure up to 2 feet high. Originally, it was the route for religious pilgrims to Machu Picchu. A powerful incentive was needed to cut, transport, and lay heavy stone this high up without the benefit of carts or wheeled apparatus. Laborers who built the road 500 years ago are an inspiration for your daylong race. The Inca Trail is an engineering feat that eventually expanded into a 25,000-mile network across mountains, deserts, and jungles. Chasquis were Incan runners who once traveled these paths to relay important messages between villages and bring gifts to royalty.

With this history underfoot, runners begin the race following the Cusichaca River upstream for 3 miles. For those opting to leave at 4:30 a.m., an hour and a half earlier than the official 6:00 a.m. start, it provides some insurance that they meet the 3:00 p.m. cutoff time at mile 22. Early birds running in the dark notice the silence. A rushing river, your footsteps, and labored breaths are the only sounds. Footwork is challenging when you're relying on light from your headlamp and distant beacons from fellow marathoners. The route across a wooden bridge passes a small village called Wayllabamba, which can be reached at daybreak. Crowing roosters signal the morning. The smell of fresh-brewed coffee fills the air at this popular campsite for hikers. A first-aid station is usually a mile after this village.

At Llulluchayoc Valley, the climb becomes steeper, with ascents of almost 1,000 feet per mile. If climbing a narrow trail isn't enough, descending hikers with guides, porters, and mules can crowd the course. Runners press themselves against stone walls, evading hooves and the back ends of the animals, to avoid being crowded off the trail. Other competitors call out "runner!" to alert hikers and guides, hoping they'll step aside and yield the right of way. They often applaud and give words of encouragement.

Turn around and witness the spectacular views of the Llulluchayoc Gorge below, as well as the snowcapped mountains above. Runners are surrounded by more beautiful scenery in mossy woods, Amazon forests, and meadows before reaching the tree line. A climb follows, straight up to the "Pass of the Dead Woman," the first and highest summit on the Inca Trail at 13,780 feet.

Uneven, steep stairs coupled with low oxygen levels

increase the likelihood of missteps on the trail. Some hikers and runners don't look back for fear of losing their balance. You can find yourself so fatigued that you're gasping for air and literally pulling your legs up with your hands to clear the height of the risers. You'll swear that your heart is beating so hard it's pounding against your rib cage. The reward for all your hard work is a much-needed descent into the valley of the Pacamayo River. Negotiating stone steps descending almost 2,800 feet is still no easy task. And almost every step downward will mean an uphill all too soon.

Tired legs ascending the second summit thankfully pass an amazing site. The race course runs right through Runkurakay watchtower ruins perched on the edge of the mountain. Thousands of stones laid without mortar have endured 500 years of extreme weather and earthquakes in this highly seismic country. Now the watchtower plays host to a marathon. You'll also see Cordillera Vilcabamba, a mountain range with glacier-covered peaks glistening in the sun, before reaching Runkurakay Pass, the second summit at 12,631 feet.

The stretch to the third summit is much more benign, dropping 820 feet before a slight 164-foot climb. You run through a tropical cloud forest boasting orchids, hanging mosses, and flowers, then duck through a 65-foot tunnel that at first glance looks like a small cave. Incas amazingly cut this stone passageway through the mountain using no more than hand tools.

The third and last summit, at 11,975 feet, appears just before the ruins of Phuyupatamarca. The aid station here is a good place to rest while looking down at this "town in the clouds." Rain forest clouds engulfing the valley by this cliffside ruin give the impression that the town is floating on billowy white pillows.

You descend into the clouds on the final downhill to Machu Picchu, the stretch with the biggest drop in altitude, at more than 3,600 feet. Legs shaking from exhaustion must carefully negotiate more than 2,000 steps down a magnificent stone staircase. It passes Phuyupatamarca's ancient temples, baths, and fountains, once used in religious ceremonies including the ritual worship of water. Ceremonial bathwaters still flow through carved stone channels. The cloud forest is filled with exotic plants and flowers, including an amazing collection of orchids.

A 3-mile run downhill then demands a 500-foot uphill to Intipunku, or "Gateway of the Sun." Front-runners have been so exhausted here that they've climbed the stone steps on hands and knees. It is the last village on the trail with the finish line finally in sight, 1,000 feet below. The famous domed peak of Huayna Picchu towers above the ruins of Machu Picchu. It's not surprising "The Lost City" remained hidden all those years.

Runners enter a park gate where guards collect tickets and record the names of visitors. The race director provides you a ticket so you don't have to pay an entry fee. Passage is restricted after 2:00 p.m. so tourists have time to tour Machu Picchu and leave by 5:00 p.m. One year, the police refused entry to several exhausted competitors closing in on the finish. Undeterred, they followed a detour adding a couple more miles to a race that already exceeded regulation marathon distance.

The final stretch weaves though city ruins made of polished stone walls, fit so perfectly together that a knife doesn't fit between them. Building designs incorporated earthquake-resistant ideas such as trapezoidal doors and windows tilting inward from the base. Ingenuity earned Incas a reputation as the best stonemasons in the world.

Unfortunately, stones laid on the trail subjected to centuries of footsteps aren't evenly joined. Sharp edges and uneven erosion create hazards for hikers, let alone marathoners. Sharp stone corners several inches tall create quixotic obstacles throughout the course, occasionally dotted with boulders. You become as wary about lifting your feet as moving forward.

The finish line in the park can't be physically altered, even temporarily, with signs and aid stations. Runners are met by race officials dressed more like hikers, lending an informal air to the end of a grueling race. Many participants who've finished take photos after their daylong run to one of the New Seven Wonders of the World.

Finishing times vary between 6 and 11 hours. Even the most seasoned runners should plan on doubling their average marathon time and then some. One international ultra-distance runner who has run 50 miles in 6:40:00 clocked a similar time in this 27.5-mile race.

In the past, only three water stops and aid stations have been stationed on the course. You'll need more frequent hydration at these altitudes, so carry plenty of your own water. Maps of the race course are provided, as it's not uncommon to veer off course, especially in the rain forest.

Runners have quit due to altitude sickness since the air

has a fraction of the oxygen available at sea level. "Pass of the Dead Woman" on the first summit is the point of no return, so once you're there you'll have to keep following the trail to Machu Picchu despite having dropped out of the race.

Participants have experienced shortness of breath, sore throats, and severe headaches from altitude. Hypothermia is a hazard, especially on cold, windy mountain passes. Same-day temperatures can range from 32 degrees Fahrenheit on the mountaintops to 80 degrees Fahrenheit in the valleys, making insulating layers essential. Freezing temperatures have also solidified energy gels, so keep them close to your body heat.

Runners can carry a backpack equipped with emergency equipment such as a head lamp, food, waterproofs, and thermal Mylar survival blankets. Although an emergency pack isn't mandatory as in some other high-altitude races, it's still a good idea here.

Locals are known to chew on coca leaves or drink coca tea as a home remedy for altitude sickness. Be aware that coca leaves are part of the plant from which cocaine is derived.

Porters on the trip help man aid stations. Their low wages are allocated on a trip-by-trip basis. They are grateful for items in your kit that you might leave behind and tips are much appreciated.

Marathoners exit the park to board buses returning to Aguas Calientes, the nearest town. Soothing, hot, outdoor thermal baths work wonders for muscles sore and stiff from scaling mountains and running at altitude. The baths, built into outdoor stone ledges, line up like swimming pools with spectacular mountain views. If you can convince yourself to leave the soothing water surrounded by a postcard-perfect view, a postrace dinner is held at the hotel to celebrate mastering 500 years of history.

SELF-TRANSCENDENCE MARATHON
Honor System

LOCATION: ROCKLAND LAKE STATE PARK, NEW YORK

MONTH: AUGUST

DISTANCE/AVERAGE FIELD: 26.2 MILES/900

TELEPHONE: 718-297-2556

WEBSITE: www.srichinmoyraces.org/us/races

A two-minute meditation, as opposed to the familiar air-horn start, is the first hint that the Self-Transcendence Marathon is a different kind of race. The second is sitar, flute, and cymbal music wafting through the air and the occasional mellow tone from a conch shell. A few miles under your belt and more surprises unfold that will altogether broaden your view of competitive racing.

This modest event of less than 1,000 runners draws a surprisingly wide international field. Russian, German, French, and Hindi languages weaving through race chatter is more characteristic of a major, well-known event. A handful of runners don't even resemble traditional marathoners, suited in polo shirts and golf shorts or packing weight more suited to a slow walk in the park.

Most competitors and spectators drawn to this race are devotees of Sri Chinmoy, an Indian guru who promoted inner peace and world harmony. His following, representing 60 countries, is captivated by his teachings, promulgated through meditation centers and public events, including athletic ones. Chinmoy himself was an athlete in his own right and personally blessed each marathon up until his death in October 2007. The long-term effect his passing will have on his followers and sporting events will unfold with time.

The spiritual leader spent his adolescent years as a sprinter and decathlete, which led him to establish the Sri Chinmoy Marathon Team to encourage spiritual growth through sports. *Runner's World* thought highly enough of the guru's influence over the sport to present him with a distinguished service award in 1978.

The movement sponsors races from fun runs to ultra-marathons all over the world. The longest, and perhaps oddest, is a 3,100-mile race run over 57 days on a half-mile concrete block in the Jamaica section of Queens, in New York City. Its 5,649 laps, past fire hydrants and trash cans, are recorded by women with clipboards at card tables. In 2008, 11 out of 14 runners completed the race, logging a minimum of 50 miles a day, between 6:00 a.m. and midnight, or risking disqualification.

The Self-Transcendence Marathon's flat, nine-lap course around Rockland Lake is a little less mundane, providing soothing scenery on an August summer day. Sounds of frogs croaking and the sight of lily pads floating on the water add to the calm nature of the event. Graceful swans swim by reeds waving in the gentle summer breeze. Deer grazing in the distance don't seem frightened by the pack, although it's not your average boisterous marathon event.

Participants report a far less aggressive and stressful atmosphere despite the awarding of trophies. Tranquility permeates the race, normally a charged environment with competitive juices flowing. Perhaps those pursuing inner peace outnumber hard-line runners. The competition relies on the honor system with no timing chips or race officials recording your laps. Remember, though, if there was ever a race where your karma could catch up to you, this might be it.

Repeating nine loops gets you well-acquainted with the field as well as the crowd. Many runners wore shirts with inspirational quotes from Sri Chinmoy. A favorite was "The only perfect road is the one in front of you." Chanting replaces more traditional shouts of "Go!" and "You're almost there!" from the sidelines. Spectators rhythmically pounding drums or young women singing a cappella also lift runners' spirits. So does repeatedly seeing your family and friends if they've come to cheer you on.

The abundant support staff consists of many of Chinmoy's followers. Aid stations are stocked with traditional items like water and energy drinks. Nontraditional alternatives, such as seaweed and tea, are also offered, perhaps an energy secret known by the mostly vegetarian crowd. Unusual fare like watermelon slices and other fresh fruit,

Coke, M&Ms, and bread are available. Chinmoy encouraged a vegetarian diet as well as abstaining from recreational drugs, alcohol, and sex.

When the challenge of long-distance mileage kicks in, runners adopt mantras even if they've never chanted in the past. One first-timer selected Coca-Cola as his marathon food of choice. Chanting "Get the Coke, Get the Coke," provided incentive to lap the aid station where his soft drink waited.

Despite the harmonious state of mind, there's disappointment with the finisher's medal: An adhesive sticker displays the race name and year. The August event can get hot and humid. Temperatures rise well into 80 degrees Fahrenheit, and driving summer rainstorms can force drenched runners to slog to the finish.

Postrace food resembles a barbecue, with many high marks for variety and quality. German potato salad, pasta, and hot dogs (for the nonvegetarian finishers) are among the offerings. Surrounding the course in Rockland Lake State Park, an hour north of New York City, is a 1,000-acre recreational site. Its two golf courses, two swimming pools, tennis courts, nature center, and boat launch tempt many to stay the day and celebrate with followers—of the Sri Chinmoy variety—or your own family and friends.

SWEET!

There are times when runners don't want to push themselves to the limit. That's when a race needs to be short, scenic—in a word, "sweet."

My definition of a "sweet" race is a half-marathon or less in mileage, so it's still doable without time-intensive marathon training. It may also be a great goal if I'm working my way up in mileage, or if I haven't run in a while. A second criterion is a very scenic course that's pleasantly distracting. It's twice as nice if it's in a location worth exploring on a road trip, such as a weekend in New England, in the country, or on the coast. Last, I look for events like pasta parties or postrace festivities that seem unusually entertaining and draw a sociable crowd.

People who've been racing for years know that athletic rituals change. Some keep enduring the 26.2-milers and even kick it up to ultramarathons. More often than not, competitors shorten their mileage, perhaps mixing up their routine with a variety of sports because of injuries or simply to seek another challenge. Other runners are content with short-distance races as a matter of course.

No matter what mileage you favor, you won't want to miss the competitions that follow. Running is more enjoyable when it introduces us to people and places we wouldn't normally meet and see during our daily routine. These events can prompt you to find both by facilitating putting a quick road trip on your calendar. Running by historic covered bridges, or on the Cape Cod coast are just some of the unique experiences "sweet" races have to offer. Without them the sport just wouldn't be as much fun.

CIGNA FALMOUTH ROAD RACE
Cape Cod Summer Day

LOCATION: FALMOUTH, MASSACHUSETTS

MONTH: AUGUST

DISTANCE/AVERAGE FIELD: 7 MILES/10,000

TELEPHONE: 508-540-7000

WEBSITE: www.falmouthroadrace.com

Bartenders can be as legendary as well-known watering holes. That was the case with Tommy Leonard at the Elliot Lounge, in Boston, and Captain Kid, in Woods Hole. Never one to shy away from a dare, Tommy challenged some regulars to race, bar to bar, from Captain Kid to Brothers Four in Falmouth. Ninety-eight runners showed up in a torrential cold rain on Tommy's birthday, on a Thursday afternoon in 1973, and that's how the Falmouth Road Race was born.

The next year, 400 people showed up. Tommy knew a lot of people, including Marty Liquori, renowned for the 1,500-meter run, and Bill Rodgers, then relatively unknown. Tommy talked them into running Falmouth. Rodgers unexpectedly won the race, and the next year the highly prestigious Boston Marathon. That put the Falmouth Road Race on the map. Then Tommy convinced Frank Shorter to run and he won. Upping the ante, Rodgers brought the Greater Boston Track Club. To even the score, Frank brought the Florida Track Club. Now, 10,000 people compete and as many as 2,000 renegades have crashed the race.

When the weather's sunny on Cape Cod, running the Falmouth Road Race is like a day at the beach. The starting corrals on Water Street in Woods Hole still fill up with eager competitors in front of the Captain Kid bar. Despite a packed, sell-out crowd, the atmosphere is relaxed. Passing time before the starting gun, runners window-shop the quaint storefronts or buy a cup of coffee or a bottle of water.

A charming, small ferry takes runners from Falmouth to Woods Hole Harbor for the point-to-point race, in addition to the traditional bus to the start. The six-dollar ticket sold by race organizers for the 45-minute boat ride is a great way to avoid traffic. Parking is available close to the dock. Any race-day jitters will be calmed by watching sleek hulls with full sails grace the waters off Cape Cod. The coastline view provides an offshore tour of the race course, as you literally sail to the start.

The mid-morning race follows Surf Road along the South Shore of Cape Cod. It passes sandy beaches and clam bars with picnic tables out front. The ocean breeze and ample water stations—some that offer to hose down hot runners—keep competitors cool in the summer heat.

The race winds round the base of historic Nobska Lighthouse which first warned sailors off the rocky coastline on dark nights and foggy days in 1829. In the early nineteenth century, Woods Hole's deep harbor was home to a substantial whaling industry. Ten thousand vessels a year sailed this channel between Nantucket Sound and Vineyard Sound. The present lighthouse was rebuilt in 1876.

Boats tied up in Falmouth Harbor greet runners on the home stretch. It's a bucolic sight until a short, heartbreaking uphill socks you a quarter-mile from the end of the race. A 65-foot American flag suspended midair by a high-rise construction crane flies over the finish line. It's a sight to behold, inspiring you to conquer the difficult climb, then a much-appreciated 100-yard downhill to the finish.

Although no longer ending at Brothers Four bar, now replaced by condominiums, the 7-mile race culminates with a large celebration at the finish with food, drink, and bands. To this day, the race still attracts well-known elite runners who love its history, cash prizes, and reputation for hospitality. Many residents open their homes to runners, offering their unique brand of relaxed Cape Cod kindness.

Since summer on Cape Cod is crowded, arrive extra early to avoid race-morning traffic. More than 15,000 applicants request numbers for 10,000 slots available for the

August race. Applications can be downloaded online and are mailed in with the application fee. A lottery is held for those who apply during the first two weeks of May. Results are posted online.

If you weren't selected, your check is returned with a pink slip, guaranteeing your entry for the following year. A number of slots are reserved for Falmouth residents and those raising money for designated charities. Part of the race profits are contributed to Falmouth youth athletic groups. The local high school track coach was one of the event's original organizers.

When the Elliot Lounge closed a decade ago, Tommy moved to Falmouth. Eventually, he turned over the race to a nonprofit, Falmouth Road Race, Inc. At seventy-five years old, Tommy's knees prevent him from lining up at the start. But you can't keep a legend too far from his craft or creation: Tommy still holds court at the Quarterdeck bar and restaurant, on Main Street in Falmouth, where he occasionally bartends. His reputation as a running leprechaun precedes him, regaling those who will listen about the history of the race and his own running antics. He ran the Boston Marathon in his own unique way: Every 5 miles, he'd stop at a bar along the way for a cold beer, still managing to finish the race in 3½ hours.

COVERED BRIDGES HALF-MARATHON
A Day in the Country

LOCATION: WOODSTOCK, VERMONT

MONTH: JUNE

DISTANCE/AVERAGE FIELD: 13.1 MILES/2,300

E-MAIL: Charlie.Kimbell@verizon.net

WEBSITE: www.cbhm.com

Covered bridges have provided travelers protected crossings over rivers and streams in bucolic settings for more than 200 years. The same quaint, romantic passageways are the province of a couple of thousand runners during the Covered Bridges Half-Marathon. The course passes through and around the weathered wood of several historic crossings, on a tour of Vermont filled with rustic barns and family-run general stores.

The June event takes place in three charming New England towns: Pomfret, Woodstock, and Quechee. It's an ideal summer race location. Runners are aware of its popularity— the 2,300 spots fill up in under a half hour when online registration opens 6 months in advance of the race. There are a number of spots reserved for those willing to raise money for designated charities, but they also sell out quickly.

The point-to-point course starts at the base of Suicide Six ski slope in South Pomfret. After picking up race numbers, runners while away the time sunning on ski lodge porches or grassy slopes with empty chairlifts. Plenty of socializing occurs. The field is large enough to draw a healthy cross section of competitors, but small enough to run into familiar faces. Out-of-town runners from as far away as Atlanta have met college friends, old landlords, and coworkers waiting for the race to begin.

It's glorious on a sunny morning when temperatures average 60 to 70 degrees Fahrenheit. If it's raining, bring warm, waterproof clothes, and opt for one of the last buses to the starting area since competitors are deposited at the parking lot a couple of hours early. Private car drop-offs are also allowed, but discharging passengers early avoids traffic on the two-lane road to the start that closes shortly before the race begins.

Not far from the start, the first covered bridge sits right off Pomfret Road. It's a private one no less, crossing a stream tucked back from the main road near the owner's home, by a large pasture. Covered bridges were originally built because the roof delayed erosion, extending a bridge's life span from 10 to 80 years. It also facilitated transporting cattle across rivers because the structure resembles a barn, so the livestock were more amenable to the trip.

Runners head into Woodstock, dubbed "the prettiest small town in America" by the *Ladies' Home Journal*. It hosts Middle Covered Bridge, the only passageway crossed during the race. The large crowd carefully funnels through the brown lattice framework over the Ottauquechee River, onto a road bordering the village green. On the other side they are greeted by the official race photographer. A local band plays classic parade favorites on a flatbed trailer attached to a pickup truck, decorated with red, white, and blue ribbons and balloons.

Running down Woodstock's main thoroughfare you'll see places worth a trip back. H. Gillingham & Sons is a five-generation family store. They advertise selling a diverse range of goods, everything "from caviar to cow manure." This charming town draws the most spectators. Locals turn up the volume on their car stereos and young children boogie on the sidelines, while others raucously cheer runners on.

Leaving town on mile 4, the course follows River Road, lined with farmhouses and wildflowers on long lazy stretches. Grazing cattle dot the hillsides and the road gradually changes from pavement to packed dirt.

The course is a gentle downgrade, but hills being what they are in the country, you can count on a little rolling terrain and a steep climb between miles 8 and 9. Water stops are plentiful, every 2 miles; half of them are also stocked with energy drinks. Music accompanies runners throughout the race. Performers have included jazz and rock bands, a seasoned a cappella choir, and a group of drummers imitating the off-Broadway percussion performance of *Stomp*.

The mostly shaded stretch on River Road winds round the Ottauquechee River. It guides runners toward a beautiful view of Taftsville Covered Bridge, a 190-foot worn red expanse that's the third-oldest covered bridge in Vermont. A pretty waterfall, easy access from Route 4, and the Taftsville Country Store's cool drinks on a hot day make this a perfect viewpoint for family and friends. A small-town band inspires runners up a steep hill, onward and upward to Quechee, a village where the Ottauquechee River drops 165 feet into mile-long Quechee Gorge.

Runners follow Main Street through a picture-perfect village with ducks swimming on ponds, pastures of wild-flowers, and old barns. Conveniently, just before the race ends, on the corner hangs a sign for the Strong House Spa, offering massage, injury rehabilitation, relaxation, and detoxification.

Finishers arrive at a postrace party that lasts well into the afternoon. An abundant food tent is open to all with a race number. Each registered finisher over twenty-one years old is awarded a beer from well-known Vermont brewers including Otter Creek, Long Trail, Harpoon, and Magic Hat. Simon Pearce, a renowned glassblower, provides trophies created in his Quechee studio to the winning male and female.

Despite a sellout crowd, surprisingly the town of Wood-stock isn't overcrowded on race weekend. Parking isn't difficult and last-minute accommodations are available. Chamber of Commerce websites provide booking infor-mation for charming bed-and-breakfasts, condo rentals, and five-star resort hotels: www.woodstockvt.com and www.hartfordvtchamber.com.

Although numbers and timing chips are picked up on race day, the two race directors man a card table placed near the village green to personally answer questions. They hand-draw course maps with a red felt-tip marker using the familiar tourist maps found in stores and visitor information booths. Despite a small-town Vermont location, the race attracts a field from 32 countries. Canadians road-trip south for the weekend just for the event.

Runners return annually to indulge in favorite traditions, like a pilgrimage to Barnard General Store, 20 minutes away, for homemade ice-cream shakes and hearty sandwiches. Comfort food and locally grown produce are a favorite attraction. Pasta suppers with early and late seatings are friendly and fun. The dinners have been held at Woodstock's country clubs and fine hotels in dining rooms usually reserved for weddings and other formal occasions. You'll find the country charm surrounding this race so welcoming, you'll feel like you've been running here for years.

LIKE COVERED BRIDGES?

If the romance of running through covered bridges inspires you, there are several more races you might want to try.

Swanzey Covered Bridges Half-Marathon in Swanzey, New Hampshire, takes place on Labor Day Weekend in the southwestern part of the state. You can register at www .active.com.

In Pennsylvania, the Annual Covered Bridge Classic in Atglen is an hour from both Philadelphia and Baltimore. The runs, covering 1-, 3.1-, and 10-mile distances, take place in October. You can register at www.cbcroadrace.com.

CREDIT UNION CHERRY BLOSSOM TEN-MILE RUN
Flower Power

LOCATION: WASHINGTON, DC

MONTH: APRIL

DISTANCE/AVERAGE FIELD: 10 MILES/12,000, 3.1-MILE
RUN/WALK/350

TELEPHONE: 301-320-3350

WEBSITE: www.cherryblossom.org

A delicate light pink and white blanket of cherry blossoms blooms along the Potomac River in Washington, DC, each spring. Bursting with color, the slightest breeze loosens the fragile petals, showering those below. This pallete of color, along with the city's most famous national monuments, is the backdrop for the Credit Union Cherry Blossom Ten-Mile Run and 5K (3.1-mile) Run/Walk in April.

Start/finish lines for both races are adjacent to the Washington Monument, a marble, granite, and sandstone obelisk that's the world's tallest stone structure. The 10-mile field has grown so large, there are now wave starts. Courses for both races head toward the Tidal Basin, a small inlet encircled by cherry blossom trees draping the walkways to the Jefferson Memorial and Franklin Delano Roosevelt Memorial.

The Japanese government donated the first cherry blossom trees, in 1912, to the American people in a gesture of friendship. These Yoshino varietals are very popular, widely planted all over the world. You understand why, seeing intense bursts of white and pale pink petals transform an urban landscape into a celebration of the rites of spring. Concentrations of blush blossoms, in clusters of five or six, can bloom for up to 2 weeks.

Exact timing of the flowers' peak becomes a sought-after piece of information, available from the local newspapers and National Cherry Blossom Festival website: www.nationalcherryblossom.org. The National Park Service has a horticulturalist on staff monitoring the situation, counting down the days before the buds are expected to bloom. A route change in 2008 was designed to incorporate the optimal number of cherry trees at peak color and famous monuments into the race.

Leaving the Tidal Basin, runners enjoying a spring day head down the east side of Ohio Drive. The course circles around an island containing East Potomac Park, a favorite outdoor spot for cyclists, walkers, and in-line skaters. Participants in the 5K Run/Walk turn around at 1.5 miles, retracing the course back toward the starting line.

The 10-milers continue to Hains Point, at the tip of the park, where they run under a canopy of cherry blossom trees. They are the Kanzan variety, which bloom with a longer stem and multiple layered petals, in clusters of two to five, and usually are darker pink in color. They peak about 2 weeks after their Yoshino relatives. Whether spring comes early or late, runners get pleasure from trees in full bloom somewhere along the route.

Rounding the island, runners return to the Tidal Basin, passing Jefferson Memorial. Marble columns encircling the monument's white portico lead to a bronze statute of the third U.S. president and Founding Father. Competitors retrace part of the route they ran under the blooming cherry blossoms, and continue on to Independence Avenue.

The course follows the Potomac River to the John F. Kennedy Center for the Performing Arts at mile 7, before circling back to cross Memorial Bridge. Widely regarded as Washington's most beautiful bridge, the neo-classical granite structure was designed by famed architects McKim, Mead, and White, in 1925. It stretches from the Lincoln Memorial to Columbia Island, also known as Lady Bird Johnson Park, in honor of her quest to beautify Washington, DC. Her "Committee for a More Beautiful Capital" planted hundreds of dogwood trees and thousands of flowers on the island, by Arlington National Cemetery. Rounding a traffic circle, runners cross Memorial Bridge again, passing its numerous impressive eagle sculptures and statues of men on horseback.

The final mile of the course follows Independence Avenue, parallel to the Reflecting Pool. The south end of 17th Street is where the first two Japanese cherry blossom trees were planted in 1912 by First Lady Taft and the Japanese Ambassador's wife, Viscountess Chinda. The race ends where it started, by the Washington Monument.

Known as the "The Runner's Rite of Spring," this race fills to capacity in a matter of days when registration opens in December. Runners can get an e-mail reminder 5 days prior to the opening of online and mail-in race registration. Members of Congress and their staff enter teams, adopting patriotic names. Foreign Relaytions represent a group of runners from the Senate Foreign Relations Committee.

This popular race takes place during the two-week-long National Cherry Blossom Festival. Events range from Washington dignitaries celebrating the opening, to the Smithsonian Kite Festival competition, to National Park Service Bike Tours. A backdrop of blossoms also accompanies cultural performances, nighttime lantern walks, and a full-service tea. Cherry Chit-Chat Runs are scheduled during the festival. A park ranger, leading a fun run under the blossoms, lectures on the flower's natural and cultural history.

LIKE FLOWERS?

Brightly colored blossoms can bring a runner out of winter hibernation with several runs that celebrate spring. The Cherry Blossom Marathon, Half-Marathon, and 5K is part of Macon, Georgia's rites of spring, in March: www.cherryblossommarathon.com.

Apple blossoms are the favorite flower at the Apple Blossom Sun Trust 10K in Winchester, Virginia, in May: www.thebloom.com. Also blooming in May, the Apple Blossom Half-Marathon, 10K, and 5K in Hastings, Minnesota, near St. Paul: www.carpenternaturecenter.org/appleblossom.

If wildflowers are more to your liking, try the Mountain-to-Meadows Half-Marathon and 5K Fun Run on Lolo Pass, in June, at the Idaho/Montana Border: www.RunLoloPass.org.

FLEET WEEK HALF-MARATHON
Naval Base Race

LOCATION: NORFOLK, VIRGINIA

MONTH: OCTOBER

DISTANCE/AVERAGE FIELD: 13.1 MILES/1,500

TELEPHONE: 757-433-2054

WEBSITE: www.discovermwr.com/fleetweekhalf/fwhm.html

Civilians normally aren't allowed to run around military bases, but an exception is made for runners at the Fleet Week Half-Marathon, held the second week in October. The course is at Naval Station Norfolk, in Norfolk, Virginia, the largest naval complex in the world. Home to more than 75 ships and submarines, race scenery includes massive aircraft carriers, amphibious assault ships, destroyers, and submarines. Active-duty servicemen comprise half the field.

The race begins at 8:05 a.m. sharp under a large American flag by the parade grounds. There is no prerace fidgeting when a band in military uniform plays the National Anthem. Runners are so attentive you can hear a pin drop. An admiral signals the start with an air horn, sending the field toward the aviation side of the base.

The course is routed by runways where air operations oversee more than 100,000 flights a year, or about one every 6 minutes. Depending on maneuvers, runners have the chance to see F-18 fighter planes and C-5 cargo planes, the largest in the world. E-2s are advanced electronic planes based here. Equipped with radar domes, they resemble a smaller version of an AWAC, with folding wings for easier storage on aircraft carriers.

Past the runway, the flat course passes ramps built for seaplanes, when these aircraft were used for reconnaissance and antisubmarine warfare during World War II. At mile 8, a collection of memorials line the bay. The USS *Iowa* Memorial honors the lives of 47 servicemen lost in a 1989 training exercise. The USS *Cole* Memorial stands in memory of the 17 sailors lost in the Port of Yemen terrorist attack.

One mile more and aircraft carriers and other vessels in the United States Atlantic Fleet come into view. Norfolk Naval Base homeports 75 ships for maintenance and training, and accommodates the crew on furlough time with their families or on occasions like Fleet Week. Depending on rotation, you could be dwarfed by the USS *Dwight D. Eisenhower,* USS *Theodore Roosevelt,* or USS *Harry Truman.* Longer than three football fields, the massive gray behemoths each measure 1,092 feet, and are more than 24 stories high, keel to mast. Aircraft may be on the flight decks along with servicemen cheering on runners.

Destroyers fitted with cannon turrets on deck are escorts for aircraft carriers. Amphibious assault ships docked nearby have gated sterns to off-load tanks and troops. Submarines are also likely to be in port. After the race, tours are available on selected vessels for those holding or escorted by someone with a Department of Defense identification card.

The finish line is back at the parade grounds. Here you're decorated with your finishing medal by Navy personnel in uniform. One year, an aircraft carrier was pictured on the medal. A barbecue and entertainment follow the race.

Fleet Week Half-Marathon is a young event, first run in 2006. In its inaugural year, a state half-marathon record was set at 1:03:34.40 by Kenyan runner Wilson Chebet. Its popularity is growing, and the race field has already tripled with current registration at 1,500 competitors.

The race is organized by Navy MWR, the Morale, Welfare and Recreation Division. MWR spans all military branches, providing recreation, social, and community activities for active-duty, reserve, and retired Navy families. Military precision permeates the race, from website links with details on pacers and travel information, to manned and well-supplied aid stations, prepared to greet runners with enthusiasm no matter how far back you are in the pack.

Fleet Week festivities take place on some of the eleven bases in the area; nonmilitary personnel can access several of them during the weekend. A chili cook-off contest is held between the commands of different ships. You can sample more than thirty recipes served at decorated booths. Entertaining themes have ranged from a football scenario, inviting customers to test their talents kicking a field goal, to a fire station promoting a red-hot recipe.

If chili isn't your dish, other foods are available, as well as family entertainment. A free Friday night concert at Naval Amphibious Base Little Creek has featured such classic heavyweights as the Beach Boys, Hootie & the Blowfish, Hall & Oates, Peter Frampton, and Lee Ann Womack. The half-marathon is held on Sunday, the last day of the weeklong Fleet Week Hampton Roads celebration.

THE OTHER HALF
Red Rock Country

LOCATION: MOAB, UTAH

MONTH: OCTOBER

DISTANCE/AVERAGE FIELD: 13.1 MILES /1,500

TELEPHONE: 435-259-4525

WEBSITE: www.moabhalfmarathon.org

The Other Half" 13.1-mile race was originally conceived as consolation for losing the lottery needed for the popular Canyonlands Half-Marathon. Now many consider it the better half. Amazing red rock formations surround both races, run on Highway 128, but The Other Half starts farther north than its sister race. It finishes at the Sorrel River Ranch Resort, surrounded by a thousand shades of red, brown, purple, and maroon stone, instead of Canyonlands' more urban ending in Moab.

Race numbers are easier to obtain for this event despite a field that's less than half Canyonlands' size. Due to permit restrictions The Other Half is held on a Sunday, so in this churchgoing territory fewer locals apply. You should still register early. It has become so popular with travelers that it recently sold out by race day.

The Other Half starts in an isolated spot on the highway bridge, near mile post 30, by a ghost town. Dewey, once home to a thriving river-crossing business, was abandoned after one of the longest suspension bridges in the United States was constructed in 1916. Unfortunately, historic

SWEET!

Dewey Bridge, its wood promenade reverted to pedestrian use, recently burned to the ground when a seven-year-old playing with matches at a nearby campsite started a brush fire.

When 1,500 runners take their mark on an October morning, temperatures can dip as low as 40 degrees Fahrenheit. Fire barrels dot the race start so runners can keep warm with the help of coffee and hot chocolate. Altitude contributes to the chill in the air. Despite the desertlike scenery, you're running at 4,000 feet.

Twists and turns dominate Highway 128 as it snakes its way through some of the most scenic landscapes along the Colorado River. Sandstone, sedimentary rock, mudstone, and conglomerate eroding over one billion years have created shapes seemingly carved by an artist. Towers, buttes, mesas, and other impressive formations are colored in layers of amber, rust, and tan. It's like running in a picture postcard.

Fisher Tower, on mile 9, is a series of towers, spires, and pedestals that's a popular recreation site for hiking and rock climbing. Castle Rock is nearby, a massive plateau and tower featured in many car commercials. A group of formations called the Rectory, so-named because its rocks resemble a priest and nuns, represents centuries of erosion from sun, wind, and water. The area has been filmed in movies including *Mission: Impossible, Star Wars,* and *Thelma & Louise.* Moab's motion-picture history is on display at the Museum of Film and Western Heritage, at the nearby Red Cliffs Lodge.

Rain and snow can litter the course with red rock, but

most of the debris is cleared by volunteers beforehand. Highway 128 is closed to traffic for the duration of the race, which has a cutoff time of 3½ hours, allowing for a 16-minute-per-mile pace. The generous time limit allows people to walk the course.

Running at 4,000 feet can create health issues if you're not used to the conditions. If you didn't altitude-train or are coming from sea level, you may want to arrive several days early to acclimatize. There's little humidity in these dry hills. Between this and the altitude, you'll want to drink plenty of water at the aid stations, located every 2 miles.

The race ends at Sorrel River Ranch Resort & Spa with a cookout and plenty of beer. In comparison, the Canyonlands Half-Marathon postrace party doesn't serve alcohol because it ends in a state park. Those who place in the race return home with a memento of the scenery: Trophies incorporate red rock, crowned with a figurine. Sorrel River Ranch is conveniently located and an ideal place to stay to nurse tired and aching muscles. Room availability is limited even months in advance, so reserve very early.

Women dominate the race by almost three to one. Known as a female-bonding event, many travel 350 miles from Denver to race together. Colorado's contingent is 33 percent of the field, but half of America is represented here with competitors coming from 25 states.

Organic foods grown locally are featured at the prerace pasta party, provided by a community service nonprofit,

Youth Garden Project. The prerace meal is conveniently located in the same room as race registration. Video of previous races is played for diners.

Allow as much as one hour to drive from Moab to the starting line shuttle at Gravel Park Lot. It's accessible by only one road, so it's worth it to start early to avoid traffic. Buses are also available directly from Moab.

If you're still energetic after the race, this is one of the most beautiful outdoor sports destinations in America. Slickrock Trail, world-renowned for mountain biking, covers petrified sand dunes and ancient seabeds. River rafting, climbing, and hiking are popular here, as well as four-wheel drive tours over dunes and creeks, and scenic flights.

Highway 128 is right on the border of Arches National Park, home to more than 2,000 natural sandstone arches, included the oft-photographed Delicate Arch. Canyonlands National Park, also nearby, is a tribute to the beauty erosion creates by sculpting canyons, mesas, and other natural wonders.

LIKE RED ROCK?

The Canyonlands Half-Marathon, in March, has much of the same red rock scenery as its sister, The Other Half race: www.moabhalfmarathon.org. More beautiful stone formations await you at the St. George Marathon in southern Utah: www.StGeorgemarathon.com. The popular October race has a lottery selection process, but if you've been denied a number before, "third time is the charm" with a guaranteed entry.

Outside Las Vegas, in November, is the Valley of Fire Marathon, Half-Marathon, & 10K. Located in the Valley of Fire State Park in the Mojave Desert, runners are surrounded by 150-million-year-old sandstone formations and dunes that appear to be on fire when the sun reflects off their surface: www.vofmarathon.ning.com.

Red rock, hills, and a 6,500-foot elevation are in store at the Garden of the Gods 10-Mile Run outside Colorado Springs, Colorado, in June: www.gardentenmile.com.

TEAM SPORT

You get by with a little help from your running friends, especially when you're on the same team.

Relay races are growing in popularity, selling out faster than some well-known traditional courses. It may be the location. Who wouldn't want to retrace the gold rush trail in Alaska? Or the shorter distance required, since the course is split among team members? Then again, it's a great way to plan a get-together among friends, or make new ones on teams assembled by race organizers for those coming solo.

Relay runners band together for competitive reasons, determined to place in an award category, or dress in costume and go at a slower pace simply to enjoy a good time. Whatever your inclination, the experience will provide memories of a different sort than pounding the pavement by yourself.

There's another kind of team sport race. It highlights professional sports and a reverence for the stadium that showcases the talent. These events grant you inside access to big-league stadiums, giving you the chance to display your athletic prowess. You can rush down the 50-yard line and emulate your favorite running back, or round home plate like a shortstop who has hit one out of the park. Look up and you might catch yourself live on the big screen.

More unique races are in store when you team up running with an obstacle course. There's something inherently satisfying about reaching for the top of a wall, slogging through mud pits, and crawling through man-sized pipes. The novelty of obstacles will test your endurance and bring a greater appreciation when watching video clips of military boot camps.

Whatever team sport attracts you the most, you'll have fun with friends and the different twists these running adventures have to offer.

Running Relays

KLONDIKE TRAIL OF '98 INTERNATIONAL ROAD RELAY
Gold Rush to Canada

LOCATION: SKAGWAY, ALASKA, TO WHITEHORSE, YUKON, CANADA

MONTH: SEPTEMBER

DISTANCE/AVERAGE FIELD: 110-MILE RELAY/140 TEAMS

TELEPHONE: 867-668-4236

WEBSITE: www.klondikeroadrelay.com

In 1898, the Klondike Gold Trail attracted throngs of prospectors landing in Skagway, Alaska, to hike more than 1,000 miles to gold fields in Canada's Yukon Territory. Known as Stampeders, they hauled a year's worth of supplies, including half a ton of food, and faced exhaustion, sickness, and starvation in hopes of striking it rich. Now, more than a century later, the same pass lures 1,000 runners for a 110-mile relay, retracing the grim adventure in an overnight race and the promise of running under the Northern Lights.

The journey begins with teams of runners for the ten-stage race flying into Juneau, Alaska. A ferry ride takes you north to Skagway on the same inside passage tour that many cruise ships use. Fall colors, mostly foliage of yellow hues, are intertwined with green pine trees. Bald eagles with 7-foot wingspans glide gracefully along the shore.

At Skagway, a race staging area resembles an RV park holding rented campers for over 100 teams. Categories include Mixed, Male, Female, Masters, and combinations thereof, and Junior consists of teams under 18 years of age. A shortened course accommodates a category of Walkers. Campers provide a place to change, eat, sleep, and support fellow runners. A designated team captain oversees details such as checking for the required reflective safety apparel for night running, dispensing race numbers, and coordinating with race officials.

The evening start is in waves at half-hour intervals with the fastest teams leaving last. Each send-off is celebrated by a steam engine whistle from a black locomotive on the White Pass and Yukon Route Railroad. Built in 1898, the railway climbs 3,000 feet and is an International Historic Civil Engineering Landmark.

For the next 24 hours each team member will run anywhere from a 5.6- to 16-mile section of the race. Packing a team of compatriots in a camper for the ten-stage race results in little sleep and fast friendships reminiscent of a college road trip. You'll cross the border into Canada, so bring your passport.

Run one of the first two stages and the shorter distances are more than compensated for by elevation. Stage one is 8.8 miles long with a gain of 1,490 feet. On the second stage, the 5.6-mile stretch rises 1,752 feet—it's enough to make you wish you took the train. Little consolation is derived from the fact that they're among the only segments run in daylight.

Klondike Highway, known as Alaska 98, is so far north the road signs depict the stars in the Big Dipper. Competitors run on a narrow shoulder on the two-lane route in the same direction as traffic. Fortunately, besides the campers few vehicles venture this far.

RVs offer all-inclusive support, supplying the bathrooms, minor first-aid stations, and course spectators, albeit they're your team members. The vehicle is slowly driven alongside the runner. Headlights guide your footsteps in the pitch-black night, so it's important to have someone alert at the wheel. Stationed in the passenger seat, another team member lends a helping hand. Window down and arm outstretched, he or she holds out water bottles, a towel, tells jokes, or provides whatever else is needed at the moment.

Toward the end of a stage, the camper drives ahead to the transition point. The next runner exits, ready to be team-tagged and begin the next leg of the journey. Team members witnessing the exchange provide the cheering section. A few small towns dot the highway where campers are restocked with supplies before catching up with their en route runner.

Each station at the nine transition points has a theme. Times are recorded by race officials who can be costumed like angels in heaven, or bats, as if celebrating Halloween. Although September daytime weather averages 55 degrees Fahrenheit, at night it can drop close to freezing. Steel drums with wood-burning fires warm checkpoint personnel, as well as team members waiting for their compatriots.

As the sun sets and blankets of stars streak the sky, rolling hills replace the drastic elevations experienced on the first two stages. Runners, though, must face longer distances, up to 16 miles. If you've never run in the middle of the night you may be surprised how your body reacts compared to a morning road race. Fatigue occurred more easily for me, but I did not get out of breath. Rather, my muscle strength lagged and each stride felt less energetic than my typical race.

Up in the Yukon, most of the roads are not lighted, nor are any towns close enough to provide a light source from homes, stores, or public facilities. Desolate roads straddled by forests and lakes force you to be wary of wildlife—that includes bears, both black and grizzly. My year, a bear was sighted by a team member in a camper. The word "bear" was passed back from runner or driver down the chain of the race. Given the circumstances, it was ironic that when one runner overtook another on the course, the popular term was "roadkill."

Grizzly bear sightings during the 25th Klondike Road Relay prompted the starter to warn participants before sending out the next wave of competitors. Still, an unwitting runner on stage two had a close call. A motor-home driver tried to alert him to the proximity of the 1,000-pound beast. The runner, ears plugged with his iPod, mistakenly thought he was offered a beer instead of being warned about a bear. "No, I'm good," he replied. Eventually, the grizzly gained ground and playfully ran beside the runner. He was unaware of its presence until a competitor pointed it out. Stumbling, he felt the bear's whisker on his thigh and the heat from its breath, then ran faster than he thought possible. Police drove to the scene, but reported that the day was so foggy that they'd even miss someone being eaten on the side of the road.

My less eventful year, I ran stage five, a 14-mile leg at about 2:00 a.m. Far from civilization, a mountain slope rose on my left and Tutshi Lake stretched for miles to my right. Bottom-heavy bears can't speed down a mountain or they'll fall and tumble downhill. The odds of one swimming up from the lake were probably low, improving my chances for a bear-free stretch.

After much insisting, my team agreed to drive ahead

about a quarter mile. A full moon glistened on the still lake beside me. Like a mirror, it reflected enough light to allow me to find my way. It was early in the season for a glorious Northern Lights display (but not for the 2008 race) and a full moon would likely have washed it out. Yet the moonlit lake, the black shadow of pine trees crawling up the mountains, the stillness of the night, and the camper's taillights waiting for me in the distance, years later remain fond memories.

A bright, orange sunrise signals a return to daylight running for the final stages and the finish line in Whitehorse, Canada. Locals look forward to this annual event. After a postrace meal at the high school gymnasium, many teams continue the party at the homes of friends in town. Hospitality from strangers is everywhere. Our East Coast team knew no one out there, yet we were adopted by a local family that shared its hot tub, a cooler full of beer, and food.

An early-morning finish allows ample time to drive back to Juneau the same day. Some teams choose to camp out since there is the convenience of having the camper. Those flying to the Lower Forty-eight usually have flight schedules that keep them around for several extra days. Since many have flown far, it's worth it to continue to explore the wonders of Alaska, especially during daylight hours.

MYOMED RAGNAR RELAY NORTHWEST PASSAGE
Coasting with Friends

LOCATION: BLAINE TO LANGLEY, WASHINGTON

MONTH: JULY

DISTANCE/AVERAGE FIELD: 187-MILE RELAY/300 TEAMS

TELEPHONE: 801-295-5536/877-837-3529

WEBSITE: www.ragnarrelay.com/northwestpassage/index.php

Ragnar Lodbrok, a Nordic hero, was a pirate, conqueror, wanderer, and wild man who plundered Paris in the ninth century. Accounts of his life, based on Viking myth, are sketchy. What better namesake for a race where partners in crime traverse the Northwest Passage on a 24-hour running relay that's sure to produce a few tall tales?

The seaside town of Blaine, 110 miles north of Seattle, on Puget Sound, right by the Canadian border, is the starting point for the race. Ten to twenty teams at a time line up for a staggered start, beginning at 8:00 a.m.; fastest teams go last. Teams of 12 send off their lead runners, and then divide up into two support vehicles. Van 1 supports the first 6 team members currently on the road, supplying water, snacks, and words of encouragement at makeshift stops along the road. About a mile before the runner finishes his leg, van 1 drives ahead to the transition point, drops off the next runner, waits to pick up the finishing teammate, and then repeats this process for a total of six legs. Van 2 leapfrogs ahead to a major exchange point with runners 7 through 12, to perform the same exercise.

The four-tire routine is repeated for thirty-six legs as runners head south, down two-lane roads on the lush, green Pacific Northwest coast. Bands, massages, and sponsor giveaways for answering trivia questions (such as "Who was Ragnar?") are nice surprises found at major exchange points. At night, more practical elements are added, such as campgrounds (bring your own tent) to catch some shut-eye, a spaghetti-and-meatball meal, or a coffee stand. An hour before dusk up to an hour after dawn, runners are required to wear a team-provided reflective vest and head lamp, or carry a flashlight. Get caught without them and you will be disqualified.

Each team member runs three legs of the race, ranging between 3 to 8 miles. A runner can increase or decrease the number of legs they run; rules don't restrict team substitutions. If the drop-off routine confuses you, especially in the middle of the night, the website provides maps indicating when each team member runs. The eighteen switch-offs per van and short-distance legs result in repeatedly getting in and out of your vehicle to run or support team members, all through the day and night.

The route travels by coastal towns such as Birch Bay, and the back roads of the city of Bellingham. Caravans of relay teams cross Fidalgo Island, through Anacortes, home to Washington's largest fishing fleet and an artists' enclave. Crossing Puget Sound over Deception Pass Bridge, a popular spot for photographers, runners get a full 46-mile tour of Whidbey Island, although some of it is before sunrise. The competition ends on the southern tip, in the bucolic town of Langley. Your team ends the race together, meeting

500 feet before the finish to run through the chute toward the postrace party, with a live band, barbecues, and much-needed outdoor showers.

Networks of running friends assemble teams with a designated captain who arranges logistics and entry fees. Those who want to join a group can post a running profile on www.iamragnar.com with details like minutes per mile and whether you want to run a competitive race or just want to have fun (almost 90 percent of the field).

Enthusiastic groups dress up in costume. Teams have run in elaborate pirate costumes, complete with eye patches, three-corner hats, and cardboard daggers. Many prizes are awarded: Nom de Plume, for best team name; Far Out Fashion Award, for best team costume; and Pimped Out Van, for best decorated vehicle, are a few of the contests.

Creative juices get flowing when thinking up award-winning team names, such as "Rapid Thigh Movement" and "WHOR—Women High On Running." Vans have been decorated and dubbed "Giant Killer Rabbit," complete with 5-foot-high bunny ears, or labeled, "In My Dreams, I'm a Kenyan."

Friends have used Ragnar Relay events as an excuse for a long-deserved reunion, or opportunities to raise money for charities. After one man lost most of his family to a drunken-driving accident, friends convinced him to participate and raise money for MADD, Mothers Against Drunk Driving. Team categories include Men, Women, and Mixed divisions. The relay is structured to attract runners of all different abilities. Seventy-five percent of participants are repeat customers in the Ragnar Relay Series.

The well-organized website includes "To Do's." It out-lines procedures such as how designated captains should share information with their team. A Race Bible details rules, tips, course maps, and logistics. You're asked to place one in each team vehicle. Suggested training schedules are also included, as well as a travel agent if you need one. Arrangements with a rental-car company offer discounted rates for vehicles.

ADDITIONAL RAGNAR RELAYS

If piling friends into a van for an all-night run appeals to you, Ragnar offers relay races across America. Locations include routes in Arizona; Florida; Wisconsin to Minnesota; Texas; Utah; and Maryland to Washington, DC. New races are planned for Boston, Las Vegas, Louisville, Los Angeles, St. Louis, and New York. Visit their website, at www.ragnar relay.com.

NIKE HOOD TO COAST RELAY
The Mother of All Relays

LOCATION: MOUNT HOOD TO SEASIDE, OREGON

MONTH: AUGUST

DISTANCE/AVERAGE FIELD: 197-MILE RELAY/ 1,000 TEAMS

TELEPHONE: 503-292-4626

WEBSITE: www.hoodtocoast.com

Twelve thousand participants line up at the Timberline Lodge, on Mount Hood, the tallest peak in Oregon, the weekend before Labor Day. They're headed 197 miles down to the seashore, to run in what's arguably the largest relay race in the world, or what organizers prefer to call "the mother of all relays."

Teams are composed of 12 people, each running three legs of varying lengths to the finish, which must all be completed in 31 hours. In a two-vehicle caravan, van 1 shadows the first 6 competitors, switching off runners at transition points. Van 2 repeats this routine for runners 7 through 12.

Teams often adopt names and brightly decorate their vehicle with pictures, colored markers, and streamers. A group of women adopted "Sweet Assets" as their moniker and a group of lawyers called themselves "Dead on Arrival." Although there aren't cash awards, prizes are awarded to the best name and van design, voted on by the 1,000 teams. Food and water is self-provided. There are no aid stations on the race course, although breakfast, for a fee, is provided at a major exchange point.

Distances average from 3.5 miles to 7.8 miles on varying terrains that can include steep uphill or downhill climbs. Novices, revelers, or those who didn't train, can feel that the mileage is much longer. At an altitude of 6,000 feet at the starting line, the first leg is a serious downhill, dropping 2,000 feet in approximately 6 miles. The Friday morning race has a wave start. Twenty teams leave every 15 minutes, according to an average of their self-reported 10K times.

The scenery is spectacular as teams snake their way down from Mount Hood into the city of Portland. The course follows serene forest roads before branching off toward the coastal town of Seaside. The overnight race leaves little time for sleep, despite spaces at major checkpoints to lay out your sleeping bag (no tents allowed) every seventh leg of the journey. At the finish line a beach party is held, including bonfires, live music, food, a beer garden, and more team bonding.

The prospect of getting exercise, being social, and beautiful scenery on an all-night van ride is increasing in popularity when people make their vacation plans. Hood to Coast has sold out in a matter of hours on the first day of registration for almost a decade. This has led people who've had to join other relay races to wear T-shirts imprinted "Hood to Coast Reject." It's also led to what participants say are crowded roads and half-hour waits for the portable bathrooms at transition points.

Teams with a member living within a 50-mile radius of Portland are expected to provide 3 race day volunteers. A race manual documents course maps, race details, and rules. Dusk-to-dawn segments require wearing reflective gear and head lamps.

The race was founded by Bob Foote, an architect and marathon runner who wanted a challenge. He paired two beautiful places near his hometown of Portland with a race that he could enjoy with his friends. The inaugural event took place in 1982, and rapidly proceeded to take on a life of its own.

LIKE RELAY RACES?

If an overnight relay race sounds like fun, but you're on the East Coast, try the Reach the Beach Relay, from Franconia to Hampton Beach, New Hampshire, in September: www.rtbrelay.com. It also sells out well in advance of the race.

In Colorado, the Wild West Relay adds a Western flair to overnight relay runs. Held in early August, teams travel from Fort Collins to Steamboat Springs: www.wildwest relay.com.

If history is your passion, American Odyssey, in April, is a new 24-hour relay race through Gettysburg, Antietam, and other major Civil War sites. After touring Pennsylvania, West Virginia, and Maryland, the finish line is by the Washington Monument: www.AmericanOdysseyRelay .com.

Stadium Runs

- -

BREWERS CHARITIES 5K SAUSAGE RUN/WALK

LOCATION: MILWAUKEE, WISCONSIN

MONTH: JULY

DISTANCE/AVERAGE FIELD: 3.1 MILE RUN/WALK/2,500

———

TELEPHONE: 414-902-4501

WEBSITE: Click on "Community" at
   http://milwaukee.brewers.mlb.com/

- -

In Pamplona, Spain, the Running of the Bulls is famous, but in Milwaukee it's the annual 5K Sausage Run/Walk that sells out every summer. Mascots of the Milwaukee Brewers baseball team, Bratwurst, Polish Sausage, and Italian Sausage race to home plate from left field during home games. They were so popular with the fans that Hot Dog, and then Chorizo, eventually joined the competition.

Brewers Charities created a 5K run/walk dedicated to their beloved food figures to benefit youth recreation and education programs. It draws a sellout crowd of 2,500 in July. Fans run with the sausages, just like at one of the home games. Don't belittle the competition—Hot Dog has run the Boston Marathon three times.

The event begins—where else?—at Klement's Sausage Haus. The route crosses the parking lot and around Ring Road, encircling the stadium before heading into Miller Park, home of the Brewers. Runners emerge on the right field warning track, the dirt perimeter that prevents players preoccupied with a fly ball from inadvertently running into the wall. Heading down the baseline, past the dugout, runners round home plate before heading out the left field exit, to the finish line outside the 43,000-seat stadium.

Entry fees include a Klement's hot dog served right after the race and a voucher redeemable for a ticket to a Brewers game. An awards ceremony presents trophies depicting the famous sausages. Age categories start as young as 12 years old and under, and up to over 70 years old for the race. Unlike most races, strollers and baby joggers are allowed on the course.

DRAFT DAY 5K

LOCATION: EAST RUTHERFORD, NEW JERSEY

MONTH: APRIL

DISTANCE/AVERAGE FIELD: 3.1-MILE RUN/WALK/1,600

TELEPHONE: 732-381-0318

WEBSITE: www.oymp.net

If football is your game, head out to the Giants' Draft Day 5K in the Meadowlands Sports Complex. It's the same day as the NFL Draft held annually in New York City. While rookies are just miles away, sweating out which teams will pick them to play professionally, over 1,000 runners are lining up outside Giants Stadium in East Rutherford, New Jersey.

The latest race route weaves in and out of the sports complex parking lots and arenas, a breeze compared to driving on these heavily trafficked roads on game days. Then runners swarm Giants Stadium, scaling the spiral ramps and the first-level perimeter encircling the field. It's a familiar experience if you've ever walked around the football stadium on game day, trying to find the section marked on your ticket stub.

Once around the promenade and back at the ramp, you run to the upper level and repeat this exercise. Up here there's a view of the New York City skyline. It's a good place to empathize with those stressed-out rookies across the Hudson River in Manhattan.

Back down the ramp and outside the stadium you're led

to the gate that opens onto the end zone. Running down-field, past the 10-, then the 20-, 30-, 40-, and over the 50-yard line, you stride over turf that you've seen only from the stands or on television. More than 80,000 seats in one of the largest NFL stadiums surround you with your larger-than-life picture above on the big screen. You can rush the finish line on the far 40-yard line.

After you're led through the chutes, you can cap off your walk underneath the goalpost with your own end zone strut. Refreshments are served and a drawing is held for some of-ficial Giants merchandise. Prizes are awarded, including winners in age group categories. A Draft Day party for fans is held several hours after the race finish. Several Giants team members attend and there are photo ops with players.

Strollers and baby joggers are allowed on the course en-abling the whole family to take part in the event. Draft Day 5K proceeds go toward The Giants Foundation, providing financial and social support for disadvantaged youths and their families.

Note: Due to new stadium construction, this race is postponed until 2010.

LIKE STADIUM RUNS?

If rushing the field on a stadium run appeals to you, here are two more races to join:

The Gupton Dodge Tom King Classic Half-Marathon & 5K and Mayor's Walk (3K) in Nashville, Tennessee, gives you three different distance choices. You can learn more about the March race at www.tomkingclassic.com.

If Chicago is your hometown, or you are traveling through

in April, try the Race to Wrigley 5K run. Click on "Community" at http://chicago.cubs.mlb.com.

Obstacle Courses

BIG SUR MUD RUN
Get Dirty

LOCATION: SEASIDE, CALIFORNIA

MONTH: MARCH

DISTANCE/AVERAGE FIELD: 5.2 MILES/1,500

TELEPHONE: 831-625-6226

WEBSITE: www.bigsurmudrun.org

If clean running isn't cutting it, you can get down and dirty at the Big Sur Mud Run. The local race is frequented by many military personnel and firefighters, often volunteers at the Big Sur International Marathon.

The race begins at Freeman Stadium at California State University at Monterey Bay, California. The 5.2-mile out-and-back course includes 2 miles of paved road, and 3 miles of trails. The first mud pit, about a mile out, contains waist-high bright orange plastic road barriers that double as hurdles. Splashing into cold muddy water that sticks to your skin and trying to keep warm is part of the challenge.

Military-training exercises are required on the course, but even armed forces personnel are hampered by the soupy mixture. One obstacle, requiring running toward a wall, grabbing a rope, and crawling up its side, is made much more difficult when mud prevents you from securing a hand grip and foothold. A series of push-ups ordered by race officials dressed in military fatigues provides civilians with a taste of what it's like to be enlisted.

A tunnel-crawl under a large net is the next mud pit to conquer. Participants are down on their hands and knees for the length of the dirt pool, avoiding mouthfuls of gray water while taking in breaths. Sludge in your eyes and ears also proves a problem for making headway on the course.

The mud is made by bringing in Dumpsters filled with dirt and hosing it down with water. It's mixed to the consistency of a thick milkshake. Slogging through the pits isn't as easy as it looks. Managing your stride is much more difficult when your running shoes are filled with muck that remains in your sneakers the duration of the race. Mud also suctions your feet to the ground. The energy required to free them can hurl you over, face-first.

Participants are warned, "You will get wet and you will get muddy." Showers are provided at the finish area, but cleaning up the race course is much more difficult. It takes hours for a construction company to fill in the mud pits with dirt that was excavated to make them and break down the obstacles on the course.

Runners can enter 5-person teams in categories for Male, Female, Mixed, Corporate, Collegiate, Military, and Public Safety. Teams take on tough name tags like "Dry Heaves" and cross the finish line together, often armlocked. Individuals can also participate, entering in a civilian or military category. A finisher's medal is awarded, but expect it to get dirty.

Urbanathlons™
CONQUERING THE BIG CITY

Rushing down avenues, scaling fire escapes, and climbing over vehicles in a race to the finish sounds like an action-adventure movie. In big cities, it's action-adventure running.

These urban races connect a runner to his concrete-and-steel environment, making it possible to tackle objects that are the very source of frustration on a typical workday.

Men's Health created these races to promote outdoor physical fitness and the lifestyle built around their magazine. Registration is available for individuals or a 3-person relay team that passes the timing chip to one another. Team categories include single-sex and co-ed teams. Race proceeds go toward the Challenge Athletes Foundation.

MEN'S HEALTH URBANATHLON™
Better Than Public Transportation

LOCATION: CHICAGO, ILLINOIS

MONTH: OCTOBER

DISTANCE/AVERAGE FIELD: 10.5 MILES/1,000 INDIVIDUALS/
200 TEAMS

TELEPHONE: 800-599-5177

WEBSITE: www.menshealthurbanathlon.com

Y̶ou'll be able to eat Chicago's famous deep-dish pizza without guilt after completing the Men's Health Urbanathlon. The 10.5-mile obstacle race is a couple of miles longer than the New York City version, but the crust on that pizza is *really* thick.

Grant Park, also known as Chicago's front yard, hosts the starting line at Upper Hutchinson Field. Dressed in fatigues, a fitness expert and war veteran has sent off competitors by hollering orders. Contenders run 3.4 miles north through the park. Navy Pier is the first of four obstacles, placed near city landmarks. Runners hurdle 4-foot-tall barricades, then skin their knees crawling through 20-foot-long cement culverts. Watch out for human bottlenecks in these circular pipes, the kind that is laid in underground tunnels. Shield your face from backed-up bottoms and feet.

After a 2-mile sprint, another crawl is in store. Two Dodge trucks are raised high enough for competitors to snake under. Get up from the ground and reach for a row of monkey bars. Hand-over-hand advancement gripping the steel, and lifting your full body weight, isn't easy. If you're not competing for a prize, after several failed attempts you'll be allowed to move on.

Lake Michigan laps at your feet on a 4.5-mile waterfront run around Soldier Field Stadium. Keep in mind, you'll be back. At 31st Street Beach are Marine hurdles. Five-foot-tall beams must be climbed up and over. Planted in sand, they deaden any bounce you might hope to get from your sneakers. The challenge is almost impossible if you're not much taller than the wall. Succeed and proceed 2 miles north to Soldier Field.

Ever run a stadium? Literally, it's climbing the steps inside a stadium. Soldier Field, home of the Chicago Bears football team, has four levels holding 61,500 seats. Run upstairs to the nosebleed section's vomitorium, then climb the cement stairs and enjoy the view from the highest row. You'll appreciate the nickname "the cheap seats." On fatigued legs you climb back down the alphabetized rows, run the venue's perimeter, and exit the opposite side. Now you know why it's called Soldier Field.

Just a half-mile run and you're at your final destination, but there are two more obstacles to overcome. Two yellow cabs parked hood-to-hood force you to trample the front end of the vehicles. If you've ever been stuck in traffic with a cab meter running, despite fatigue you'll find motivation.

Last but not least, is an 8-foot wall with dangling ropes to grab and crawl over. Fatigue-clad fitness gurus yell advice from the sidelines. Getting your elbow over the top of the wall proves to be key.

It's just steps to the finish and free massages. The earlier you finish, the shorter the line. Breakfast foods are served at the postrace party where reggae and blues bands play. A well-deserved beer tent is also on the premises for a run well done.

MEN'S HEALTH URBANATHLON™
Better Than Public Transportation

LOCATION: NEW YORK, NEW YORK

MONTH: SEPTEMBER

DISTANCE/AVERAGE FIELD: 8.1 MILES/800 INDIVIDUALS/100 TEAMS

TELEPHONE: 1-800-599-5177

WEBSITE: www.menshealthurbanathlon.com

Ever get stressed by traffic in the Big Apple? This is your chance to rule the streets. The New York Men's Health Urbanathlon combines running and mastering a military-like obstacle course in the heart of the city. After you finish the course, you may feel like you're ready to join the Marines.

The New York City race begins in Central Park, heading west to the bike path. Pier 84 holds the first challenge, a barricade and culvert crawl.

You know those annoying waist-high bright orange barriers that detour you at construction projects and events? Now is your chance to jump a line of them like a hurdler at the Olympics. Next are white culverts, or pipes, large enough to fit a human. You crawl through a couple while trying to avoid being kicked by the competitor in front of you. When you're through the tunnel, it's back on the bike path for a 1.5-mile run.

Out of breath? Don't let it throw you at Pier 54. Hit the road, literally, when the next obstacle requires crawling under two Dodge trucks, angled upward to accommodate competitors of all shapes and sizes. Once out from under, you're not finished yet. Grab on to a seemingly endless line of monkey bars, and work your way forward. Lose your grip and you'll be asked to start again. Competitors not vying for a time are given a bye if they fall and are allowed to move on.

There's no rest for the weary at Pier 54. Without a break, Marine hurdles await. Hoist yourself up and over a series of 5-foot-tall walls. Both feet are required to touch the ground in between. For many competitors, especially those under 6 feet tall, it was difficult if not impossible to scale the walls. Officials offered a leg up for those who were struggling, or allowed them to bypass the obstacle altogether.

It's back on the bike path for a 2.5 mile sprint down to the newly reconstructed World Trade Center 7, where runners take on 52 flights of fire stairs. Competitors hang on to stair rails for support even before they're halfway up the skyscraper. It was hard not to think back to September 11 and imagine what escaping danger was like in the emergency stairwells. After the trip down, you still have a 1.25-mile run to your next challenge.

The Taxi Hurdle is not an attempt to get the last ride from the airport at midnight in the rain. It's trampling the roofs of two yellow cabs parked hood-to-hood. Watching competitor after competitor add to the dents in the hood will leave you wondering who volunteered their vehicles.

Last but not least, you scale that infamous military-base wall climb seen in the movies. Grab a rope and walk your feet up and over, then jump to a platform midway on the other side. Race officials man the wall, prepared to provide a lift up to help you complete the trajectory.

Fatigue can cause competitors to stumble past the end of this 8.1-mile race. Mileage includes the 52-floor stair climb and descent. If you have energy left, postrace festivities and award ceremonies are a mile away at South Street Seaport. It's a nice walk past the Staten Island Ferry terminal.

A tall ship is docked at the pier with food, festivities, and fun. There are football and basketball tosses if you're still in the mood for competion. Break-dancers, skateboarders, and other urban entertainers demonstrate for the crowds.

MORE OBSTACLES?

There's been talk of extending the Men's Health Urbanathlon to other cities, such as San Francisco. One international offering is already being held in the Philippines. For race updates, check the website at www.menshealthurbanathlon.com.

TOURIST ATTRACTIONS

Races are held in a dazzling array of international cities. The long-standing World Marathon Majors, known for large prize money and five-figure fields, include Boston, New York City, Chicago, London, and Berlin. These cities now offer half-marathons, too, to satisfy the increased popularity of shorter-distance racing. Cosmopolitan destinations such as Paris, Rome, and Athens, also have 26.2- and 13.1-mile events—I can't think of many runners who wouldn't want to visit the Eiffel Tower postrace.

Proven a great way to attract tourist dollars, races in interesting places are all over the world and worth exploring. Running through the middle of the twelfth-century temples at Angkor Wat, in Cambodia, is a race a fraction of the age of the Paris Marathon. Yet it's one that deserves its own bragging rights. Other intriguing races have been around for as long as the cosmopolitan models; they're simply undiscovered. The thirtieth running of the Intercontinental

Istanbul Eurasia Marathon in Turkey is the only marathon I know that takes you across two continents.

I'm a fan of traveling off the beaten path and adding competitions with smaller fields or unusual locations to my running wish list. Races in unusual places have taken me beyond the hotels, restaurants, and tour buses on an average vacation, and to countries where I normally wouldn't have made it a priority to travel.

Off-beat foreign marathons made me an immediate member of a group of international runners with whom I discovered I had a lot in common. Signing up with travel packages operated outside the U.S. put my nationality in the minority, granting me an even broader perspective on international relations.

Whether you're traveling alone, with a fellow runner, or with a companion who doesn't even exercise, there's a race embedded in an interesting culture that's worth exploring. Most packaged trips include a tour, and schedule the run near the beginning of the trip. Then there's enough time to get rid of pre- and postrace anxiety, and save the rest of the trip for touring.

I try to remind myself to make progress every year on the checklist of places I want to see in my lifetime. And after all that training, I don't have to worry about trying all those local delicacies. Consider packing your sneakers in your suitcase and make your next vacation really worth remembering, by running in one of the following foreign countries.

ANGKOR WAT MARATHON
Cambodian Temples

LOCATION: ANGKOR WAT, CAMBODIA

MONTH: NOVEMBER/DECEMBER

DISTANCE/AVERAGE FIELD: 26.2 MILES/20, 13.1 MILES/800,
6.2 MILES/400, 3.1 MILES/600

TELEPHONE: 619-298-7400

WEBSITE: www.kathyloperevents.com/angkorwat
or www.angkormarathon.org

Circling a massive temple, buried for centuries under dense jungles, provides ample distraction during a long race. Thousands of stone carvings decorate Angkor Wat, including apsara, which are heavenly nymphs, and devatas, or guardian spirits, which can lift morale when you're physically exhausted. The twelfth-century shrine is part of a larger complex of outlying temples at Angkor, ("city" in Sanskrit) covering 400 square miles. What was once the largest preindustrial city in the world is now your race course.

Transportation from your hotel on race morning might be provided by a tuk-tuk, a three-tire taxi that resembles a rickshawlike automobile. Negotiating a rate beforehand avoids disputes, and be armed with a map confirming your destination. Travel to the start is before daybreak. Arriving on-site at sunrise, Angkor Wat's rounded towers stand in contrast to red and purple hues in the morning sky.

The starting line for the 13.1-mile loop is by the moat,

measuring 3,280 feet around, that guards Angkor Wat. Built by King Suryavarman II, the temple's famous towers are designed after Mount Meru, home of the Hindu gods, and are proudly depicted on the Cambodian flag. This architectural wonder is the most famous and best-preserved temple on the grounds. Runners circle halfway around it before heading toward Banteay Kdei. This dilapidated monastic complex hasn't withstood the test of time as well as Angkor Wat. Piles of sandstone blocks are scattered over its grounds.

The course passes Ta Prohm, one of Angkor's most popular temples. Silk cotton tree roots cascade down its weathered gray exterior. Surrounding jungle adds to its exotic charm. It's so photogenic that competitors have stopped to take pictures.

Continuing past Ta Keo, an incomplete temple built in 1000, runners are led to the much larger complex of Angkor Thom. They race through the aptly named Victory Gate, the entrance through which King Jayavarman VII would ride into the enclosed capital city after a successful battle. The course is routed through the ancient metropolis, passing major tourist attractions, such as the Elephant Terrace. Thought to be an assembly point for troops, elaborate carvings of elephants and trunks line the walls. The city's state temple, the Bayon, has masses of carved faces from stone-block mosaics that are a site to behold.

Runners attract the attention of locals, many of them children. Clapping and cheering, they hold out their hands for high fives and giggle at the spectacle of runners circling the course. The event raises awareness and money for victims of land mines scattered throughout the country, left by the Khmer Rouge. The political party's rule from 1975 to 1979 under Pol Pot resulted in the deaths of one-fifth of the country's population through execution, starvation, and forced labor. Cambodia has one of the highest percentages of land mine casualties worldwide, and over half of the victims are children.

The Angkor Wat Marathon is held by tour operator Kathy Loper Events in conjunction with the Angkor Wat International Half-Marathon. Looping the half-marathon course twice completes an official 26.2-mile marathon distance.

The Angkor Wat International Half-Marathon, organized by a Japanese race director, includes 10K (6.2 mile) and 5K (3 mile) distance races, attracting competitors from 39 countries. A 3K kids race is also available. A 21K wheelchair race includes athletes affected by landmines.

The prerace pasta party serves traditional Cambodian fare. Spring rolls, curry dishes, and noodles are abundant. During dinner, runners are entertained with traditional apsara dances. Similar to the stone carvings, apsara (heavenly nymphs) danced for the royal court to welcome the Thai gods into a temple. Dancers and their delicate movements, considered one of the culture's highest artistic achievements, were targeted for extermination under the Khmer Rouge. The few survivors taught new generations this coveted tradition.

Most competitors stay in Siem Reap, the closest town to Angkor, almost 200 miles from Cambodia's capital Phnom Penh. A race tour package will smooth your travel arrangements, ensure your race entry, and book you into first-class hotels.

If you prefer a less expensive trip, there's adventure in store if you fly to Bangkok. There, you can take a train or hire a taxi to take you to the Cambodian border. After clearing customs, a 6-hour rickety bus or 4-hour taxi ride, on 100 miles of potholed roads, takes you to Siem Reap, where you can find accommodations and race-day transportation.

GREAT WALL MARATHON
1,000 Years of History Under Your Sneakers
LOCATION: JIN SHAN LIN, CHINA (100 miles northeast of Beijing)
MONTH: SEPTEMBER
DISTANCE/AVERAGE FIELD: 26.2 MILES/75, 13.1 MILES/30,
    6.2 MILES/35

TELEPHONE: (Germany) +49-89-43-03-143
WEBSITE: www.greatwall-marathon.com

Nothing captures the romance of running like wearing down your sneakers on 1,000 years of history on the Great Wall of China. Stone steps of different shapes and sizes—60,000 in all—are hardly detectable when you look at this beautiful, seemingly unending ancient architecture undulating over countless hills. But there's no doubt they're there when you climb this world wonder, built during the Ming Dynasty to keep out pillaging nomads.

The course, never flat and always tricky, requires strict focus on foot placement. Wide stone walkways resembling large terraces have a small riser every 10 feet. They lead to stairways in corridors so narrow that I pressed myself against the stone wall, enabling runners coming in the opposite direction to pass on the four-loop course.

Lookout towers hiding steps as tall as my knees required scaling to the roof, then climbing up stick ladders, and crawling through windows. Ledges less than a foot in width had to be shimmied across to avoid stone pits. The creative course was delightful. I felt like a kid on a jungle gym.

Volunteers, wearing sunglasses, staff water stops at 3-mile intervals. Sitting under beach umbrellas, stationed on the Wall's lookout towers, they escaped the 80-degree-Fahrenheit heat, while recording the names of runners coming and going. There are no portable toilets provided on the course, requiring participants to climb off the Wall at choice locations, if the need arises.

Centuries of decay have left small stones and dust as the only foothold on portions of the course, a hazard pointed out to us by full-time architect and part-time race organizer Wichart Hölscher. Hölscher showed us his renderings and blueprints of the course at a briefing in Beijing, the site of race registration and accommodations. He has coordinated this race, as a hobby, every year since 1996, save 2003 due to the SARS outbreak in China.

The fancy footwork, commanding total concentration for the entire marathon, left me exhilarated for hours after the race. Cross-training to master the never-ending stair climbs is a good idea. I was glad that I had worked out with weight machines at the gym. Since the race director/tour operator is German, so are most of the competitors, al-though runners represent more than 15 countries.

The slower you race, the bigger fan base at the finish, since everybody travels on buses almost 3 hours to and from the race start. There is no official finishing time, but coming in last is memorable. You'll have the entire field clapping and waving you in. They can follow you from a half-mile away, as you traverse the top of the Wall toward the finish. Waiting for others to end the race, runners snacked on packed lunches and took pictures of friends. I enjoyed a well-deserved massage on the Great Wall of China, by the hotel masseuse who accompanied us to the race. Talk about a once-in-a-lifetime experience!

Finishing times ranging from $2\frac{1}{2}$ to $6\frac{1}{2}$ hours are capped off by an awards ceremony on-site. Chinese fire-crackers are set off and the familiar theme music from the Olympics is played on a black boom box on the ancient Great Wall.

The beauty and grace of the Wall gently snakes across green rolling hills, stretching 4,000 miles to the west. It's like running in a beautiful picture. Although I'm not in-clined to repeat a course, this is one of the few marathons I'm tempted to run more than once. The field is limited to less than 100 runners to avoid unnecessary erosion on the centuries-old fortification.

Although other Great Wall Marathons exist, this is the only one I know of that's entirely run on the Wall, and that's worth selecting this race above others. Nine- and fourteen-day tour packages are available. Beijing city tours are included. Side trips are worthwhile when you've flown all the way from the U.S. mainland. Excursions to Shanghai and Xian, home to the Terracotta Army of 8,000 soldiers, dating back to 210 BC and unearthed by local farmers, are available at an additional cost.

SCALE HISTORY

If mastering the Great Wall of China is on your wish list, but you can't schedule a fall trip, try www.great-wall -marathon.com. The May race takes place partially on the Great Wall, but primarily in the surrounding countryside.

INTERCONTINENTAL ISTANBUL EURASIA MARATHON
Two Continents for the Road

LOCATION: ISTANBUL, TURKEY
MONTH: OCTOBER
DISTANCE/AVERAGE FIELD: 26.2 MILES/700, 9.3 MILES/1,800

TELEPHONE: (Istanbul) +90-212-453-30-00
WEBSITE: www.istanbulmarathon.org

Istanbul, the only city in the world to straddle two continents, is naturally the only marathon run on two continents. The race is held during Turkey's Independence Celebrations. The marathon begins on the Asia side, near the Bosphorus Bridge which guides runners into Europe, over a mile-long span across the strait. On the other side of the bridge, more sights await you in this history-rich city dating back to 667 BC.

Once the capital of the Roman, Byzantine, and Ottoman empires, today Istanbul is the largest city in Turkey. City views, along the coasts of the Mediterranean and Black Seas from the Bosphorus Bridge are stunning, but the fall winds can chill you to the bone. With temperatures averaging 46 degrees Fahrenheit this time of year, it has been known to snow race-day morning. Combining the start for the marathon and 15K race, which owns a much larger field, makes for a crowded crossing. The cutoff time for the marathon is 5 hours; after that, cars and trucks are allowed back on the road. In this congested city of 14 million, at the beginning of the race, it's better to stay in front of 15K runners so that nobody slows your race time.

In Europe, the course leads past the Hagia Sophia. A sixth-century marvel, it was, for 1,000 years, the world's largest cathedral, later a mosque, and is now a museum. In the fifteenth century, fortresses were built near the waterways to control shipping. These edifices and the Valence Aqueduct, which supplied the city's water in the late Roman Empire and Early Byzantine era, line the road.

The Ataturk Bridge takes runners over the Golden Horn, the halfway point where the Mosque of Sultan Ahmed glistens in the sun. Also known as the Blue Mosque, 20,000 glazed tiles adorn the walls of its interior. Before crossing the waterway again over the Galata Bridge, the course steers by the fifteenth-century Topkapi Palace, home to Ottoman sultans for more than 400 years.

Few spectators come out to watch the back half of the marathon. Many aren't aware of the event. The course is a little hilly, with gradual inclines. Water and sponge stops are frequent along the route. Runners report times when they've run out of water, so it's a good idea to carry some during the race. The finish line is at Inonu Stadium, the home of the city's soccer team, but runners don't collect their medals until they return to the race registration area.

Not many people cross two continents in one day, let alone in one marathon, a characteristic that makes this a very unique race. The big question is, if you wanted to run a marathon on every continent in the world, could you count this race·as having covered Europe or Asia or both?

THE INTERNATIONAL MARATHON OF MARRAKECH
Khalid Khannouchi Country

LOCATION: MARRAKECH, MOROCCO
MONTH: JANUARY
DISTANCE/AVERAGE FIELD: 26.2 MILES/520, 13.1 MILES/1,750

TELEPHONE: (Marrakech) +212-24-44-68-22
WEBSITE: www.marathon-marrakech.com

If you desire an exotic run down a palm tree–lined course, past traditional street markets selling everything from water pipes to watches, while dodging donkey carts and sheep, come to Marrakech. In this city of one million residents, located in southwest Morocco in North Africa, you'll be cheered on by spectators dressed in traditional Berber costumes. The country is home to Khalid Khannouchi, holder of the world-record time of 2:05:38 in 2002, after breaking his own three-year record time by 4 seconds.

In addition to a marathon, there's a "semi-marathon" (also known as a half-marathon) in this French- and Arabic-speaking metropolis. A Rollerblade marathon and a fun run are included, with entrants mostly consisting of teenagers.

The Atlas Mountains, snowcapped peaks of 12,000 feet, can be seen from the distance as runners wind their way down boulevards designed with French influences. Surrounding architecture dates back to the Middle Ages. Marrakech has an ancient part of the city, Medina, and an adjacent modern part, Gueliz. Both sections of the city are covered on the marathon race course, before heading out to the suburbs. The course also crosses the "route de Casablanca."

Although the marathon is run on city streets, runners shared their lanes with locals pushing sheep-loaded handcarts, or pulling red Radio Flyer wagons loaded with wares. Camels have also been sighted on the sidelines, looking on in curiosity. The race sometimes resembles an obstacle course, as runners dodge a large amount of car traffic and crowds. Many families are on their way home for feasts in honor of the Muslim Eid al-Adha holiday, an important date on the Islamic calendar that coincides with the marathon.

Many veiled women in this moderate Muslim country compete in their head scarves. Some cheer from the sidelines. It makes it all the more interesting when they outstretch their hands for a marathon tradition of high-fiving the runners and shouting encouraging words—in Arabic.

The January race temperature hovers at a chilly 40 degrees Fahrenheit at the start, but if you finish around noon, the temperature may become 30 degrees warmer. There's direct sun on most of the course, making frequent water stops necessary and appreciated. Sugar cubes are dispersed at aid stations, along with locally grown oranges, raisins, and dates.

Locals in full-length traditional red robes and fringe hats, sell water to thirsty runners from canvas bags full of bottles. Race officials in cars driving the course hand out water for free, distributing containers to outstretched hands. Although oranges and water are plentiful, there may be no energy bars or gels at aid stations.

There have been some concerns about race organization, including the lack of toilets, infrequent mile markers, and exhaust fumes. Cars and mopeds allowed onto the rarely traffic-free course can number so many, you may question whether you're still on route, until you spot a sign or a race official. In years past, there were no chip electronics to record runners' times. Competitors crowded sidewalks by the race start if they didn't want additional time added to their finish by starting from the back of the pack. If you're a flexible runner who doesn't get easily ruffled in foreign countries, you'll enjoy the unique atmosphere of this race. North American and European competitors are few and far between, and African entries will give you a run for your money. It's not just a marathon; the city hustle and bustle crowding the course will make this run an adventure. But how often can you say you saw a camel during your race?

TRY DUBAI!

Another course a world away where you can sight a camel is the Standard Chartered Dubai Marathon, in January. The course runs along the city's Persian Gulf coastline; 10K and 4K fun runs are also held. The marathon awards winners large cash prizes, plus a one-million-dollar bonus for a new world record: www.dubaimarathon.org.

MARABANA HAVANA MARATHON
Hot! Hot! Hot!

LOCATION: HAVANA, CUBA

MONTH: NOVEMBER

DISTANCE/AVERAGE FIELD: 26.2 MILES/700, 13.1 MILES/600, 6.2 MILES/250, 3.1 MILES/100

TELEPHONE: 800-856-4777

WEBSITE: www.cuba1tours.com/marabana/running.html
www.cubastartravel.com

Hot! Hot! Hot! That's the climate at the colorful Marabana Havana Marathon in Cuba, situated just 228 miles southeast of Miami. Despite chilly diplomatic relations with the United States, Americans have been able to apply for cultural exchanges concerning educational, health, sports, and other events. Even when you obtain the proper license from the U.S. Treasury Department, racing in Cuba still feels like you're running under the radar. It's also worth witnessing how local life was affected by Fidel Castro's 5-decade-long political regime.

The race starts at a beautiful plaza in front of El Capitolio, the seat of government in Cuba until the 1959 revolution. Ironically, it's designed after the U.S. Capitol building in Washington, D.C. The field of competitors is small for both the full and half-marathon. A poor economy is reflected in the running gear. Locals wear sneakers with thin white soles and no treads, reminiscent of Keds. Others run barefoot. Outfits range from white cotton undershirts and street shorts to sleeker attire that usually pegs competitors as foreigners.

My year, clothing didn't affect the performance of the many competitive athletes who traveled across the country to attend the event. In addition to athletic prowess, they have the advantage of being used to the heat and humidity. Temperatures can rise to 90 degrees Fahrenheit and 85 percent humidity on sun-exposed concrete that can sizzle like salsa music. The year I ran, the winner clocked in at 2:28:07, but missed his medal ceremony looking for the friend holding his bag of clean clothes. She had fainted from the heat and was taken to the hospital.

The two-loop marathon course leaves the city center, past the Museum of Revolution, once the presidential palace and now housing details of Castro's rule. Runners are routed along the Malecon waterfront where locals cast their fishing poles into the Bay of Havana. Manor houses that were much better tended prerevolution dot the route.

Much-needed water stops are unevenly spaced on the course. Long stretches of drought increase the importance of carrying your own water, given the oppressive temperatures. A little comic relief could be had when volunteers at aid stations wore T-shirts decorated with a polar bear in ice-blue waters. Water handed off in plastic bags was so tightly sealed that I resorted to tearing it open with my teeth. Most of it dribbled down my chin and chest. Drinking the much-needed liquid was difficult at best, and the sanitary handling of bags was in question. When I returned home, I got sick as a dog.

Three-foot tall, freezer-sized ice blocks intermittently stood on the side of the road, wet and glistening in malformed shapes, the result of strong sun. Jagged chunks varying in size were hacked off by men with picks and large knives, and handed off to runners. Sweaty fingers wrapped around sharp edges of ice, in various sizes, created new shapes that quickly dwindled on contact with beet-red faces, sunburned arms, and overheated chests.

Car exhaust from 1950s Chevrolets, Dodges, and Plymouths, complete with big fins, chrome grilles, and hood ornaments, proved a struggle, especially in a country without emissions standards. Buses pulling out in front of me, onto the road, spewed big, black, thick clouds of exhaust. Trailing runners were left facing a constant stream of emissions as the vehicles slowly drove ahead. Competitors complained of sore throats from the air.

The course winds past Revolution Square, the site of many political rallies. The country's socialist republic provides political scenery with signs denouncing Americans as *imperialistas*. One banner depicting a vicious Uncle Sam was located in front of the U.S. Interests Section, the substitute for an embassy in Cuba.

Runners weave in and out of traffic on a race course including cars, buses, bicycles, and Cubans whiling away a typical Sunday. People cross in front of you with baskets of flowers, dogs, or their four kids in tow. So much activity fills the streets that runners can lose sight of the course.

Despite a lack of upkeep, the city architecture is beautiful and ornate, reminiscent of historic districts in Spanish cities. Beautiful but worn, pockmarked 400-year-old colonial buildings surrounded by intricate streets further obscure the race route at the end of the loop. The small marathon field allows for competitors to be spread apart for long distances, so finding your way by looking for fellow competitors isn't practical.

On the last lap of the two-loop course, many aid stations were abandoned after running out of water or once their block of ice melted. It burdened even seasoned athletes. One veteran of the Hawaii Ironman triathlon told me, "The last 3K were the longest of my life." Originally concerned about drinking the water, his fears were overridden by extreme thirst.

At the end of the race, no overhead clock allowed exhausted runners to glance up to check their race time. Organizers ran out of medals because they rewarded half-marathoners with the same coveted ornament, disappointing those sticking it out for 26.2 miles in the grueling heat from being anointed at the finish. Water suffered the same fate as the medals at the finish, so thirsty runners did little lingering at the end of the race.

Friends indulged in postrace ice massages inside a building named "Kid Chocolate," after the Cuban boxing legend of the 1930s. Competitors on tables cooled off quickly when big chunks of ice were rubbed over their exhausted bodies.

Poverty permeates the dilapidated sports stadium where winners are announced. The traditional pasta dinner served the night before the race consisted of a half plate of over-cooked noodles topped with a tablespoon of meat sauce, vanilla wafer cookies, and hard candies, washed down with a cup of pink guava juice.

Technically, we weren't allowed to spend more than $200 U.S. a day on hotel, meals, or souvenirs. American credit and debit cards don't work in Cuba, so we carried cash. The travel embargo for Americans is an economic one. We arrived in Havana on a prop plane from Miami, where charter planes for licensed travelers can depart. To skirt the economic em-bargo, some U.S. citizens book all-inclusive travel from a third country such as Canada, Mexico, or Germany. Of-ficially, you avoid spending U.S. dollars in Cuba, although you still risk heavy fines for traveling to Cuba. Official State Department rules can be checked at: http://travel.state.gov/travel/cis_pa_tw/cis/cis_1097.html.

Despite cold diplomatic relations between the U.S. and Cuba, the locals were warm and embracing. Many Cubans would run with you on stretches of the race, trying to com-municate in broken English. Although I'm not fluent in Spanish, I could still say a few words. My American com-petitors appreciated the severe economic struggle faced by Cubans.

"Running along the ocean I thought about how many Cubans sailed into the ocean in the middle of the night to try to get to the U.S. to improve their life," said one runner. "I thought if they can withstand that, I can run 26.2 miles of a race, no matter how hot it is."

THREE COUNTRIES MARATHON
Bring Your Passport

LOCATION: LINDAU, GERMANY, TO BREGENZ, AUSTRIA, TO ST. MARGRETHEN, SWITZERLAND

MONTH: OCTOBER/NOVEMBER

DISTANCE/AVERAGE FIELD: 26.2 MILES/600; 13.1 MILES/1,400; 7.1 MILES/400

TELEPHONE: (Germany) +49-8382-260030
WEBSITE: www.sparkasse-marathon.com

Long-distance running is all the more sweet when your efforts take you on a tour—how about Germany, Austria, and Switzerland? The aptly named Three Countries Marathon begins in a corner of Central Europe at the well-known spa town of Lindau, Germany, in the Bavarian Alps, about 310 miles from Munich. The course resembles a country drive as it follows Lake Constance, the largest lake in Europe, which is surrounded by snowcapped mountains, flower-filled meadows, and quaint villages.

You won't need your passport when you cross the Austrian border to Bregenz. You run near the town wall, dating back to the thirteenth century, and pass much baroque architecture. The enchanting town is surrounded by forests, filled with wooden chalets that have come to symbolize homes in the European Alps. Mount Pfaender rises in the distance. You can see the cable car that shuttles tourists to the top, where they can enjoy a bird's-eye view of the marathon route.

In Bregenz, the course, flat as a pancake, passes the Lake Promenade, a local gathering place for philosophers, politicians, writers, and musicians. The off-highway route enhances the scenery, but it's tricky for runners weaving around one another who want to keep a steady pace. It's a bit easier after the 10-mile mark, when the marathon and half-marathon courses split.

Marathoners are off to Switzerland on their three-country tour, which lies across Lake Constance. They'll pass two picturesque villages, Rheineck and St. Margrethen, before circling back toward Bregenz. There, stretched out over the lake, is the largest open-air stadium in the world. The 7,000-seat arena is host to the Bregenz Festival every summer, staging operas, plays, and musical events. Runners also pass Mehrerau Monastery; originally settled in 611, it now houses a college staffed by monks from the abbey.

Many tourists in town greet you at the end of the race. The finish line at Casino Stadium, in Austria, ends the marathon in a completely different country from the race start. You may wonder how you get back to Germany if your baggage, car, or hotel is by the starting line. Tickets are available for a postrace ferry, crossing Lake Constance from Bregenz to Lindau, sold the morning of the race. Arrive at the ticket line early, because most of your competitors favor this return transportation. Be sure to locate adequate parking early at the race start in Lindau, because thousands of runners descend on this small city. A train ride to town is also available.

Weather for the October race in the mountains can be chilly, as low as 46 degrees Fahrenheit. Cross your fingers and hope to avoid a steady, seasonal rain, not unusual during the fall season.

Boats decorating the shores of Lake Constance host an offshore pasta party. This milk-rich region is famous for its cheeses. Kässpätzle, a local specialty of homemade noodles and cheese, is among the buffet selections. Bicycle riding, a popular pastime here, is offered to those who want to tour the race course. This unusual way of surveying the course is ideal for those who aren't worried about tiring out their legs with a 26.2-mile ride.

LIKE MULTIPLE COUNTRIES RUNS?

If you'd rather tour Italy, France, and Monaco and run along the Cote d'Azur, the Marathon de Monaco et des Riviera is in November. The race starts in front of the illustrious Monte Carlo Casino: www.monaco-marathon.com.

INDEX TO GREAT RACES

Name	Website	Mileage	Month	Temperature	Location
"BECAUSE IT'S THERE"					
Antarctica Marathon & Half-Marathon	www.marathontours.com/antarctica	26.2 13.1	February/ March	15–30°F	King George Island, Antarctica
Borrowdale Fell Race	www.borrowdalefellrunners.co.uk	17	August	53–68°F	Rosthwaite, England
Lantau Mountain Marathon	www.seyonasia.com/Koth/lt	18.5 8.7	January	55–67°F	Hong Kong, China
Mongolia Sunrise to Sunset	www.ultramongolia.com	62.1 26.4	July	54–75°F	Hovsgol National Park, Mongolia
Mount Kilimanjaro Marathon® & Summit Climb	www.mtkilimanjaromarathon.com	26.2 13.1 6.2	June	60–78°F	Moshi, Tanzania
Other Kilimanjaro Races: **The Kilimanjaro Marathon**	www.kilimanjaromarathon.com	26.2 13.1 3.1	March	66–90°F	Moshi, Tanzania
Mount Washington Road Race	www.mountwashingtonroadrace.com	7.6	June	38–50°F	Gorham, NH

Name	Website	Mileage	Month	Temperature	Location
Pikes Peak Marathon® & Pikes Peak Ascent®	www.pikespeakmarathon.org	26.2 13.3	August	39–68°F	Manitou Springs, CO
Other Peaks to Scale:					
Jungfrau Marathon	www.jungfrau-marathon.ch	26.2 2.6 1	September	52–74°F	Interlaken, Switzerland
Marathon du Mont-Blanc	www.montblancmarathon.net	26 14.3 6.2	June	54–72°F	Chamonix, France
Siberian Ice Marathon	www.sim.omsknet.ru/ice/en	13 4.3	January	−39– −12°F	Omsk, Russia
EAT, DRINK, AND BE MERRY					
Kentucky Derby Festival Marathon & miniMarathon	www.derbyfestivalmarathon.com	26.2 13.1	April	46–67°F	Louisville, Kentucky
Marathon du Médoc	www.marathondumedoc.com	26.2	September	55–75°F	Pauillac, France
Other Wine Races:					
Healdsburg Wine Country Half-Marathon	www.runhealdsburg.com	13.1	October	38–66°F	Healdsburg, CA
Napa-to-Sonoma Wine Country Half-Marathon	www.runcarneros.com	13.1	July	53–82°F	Napa, CA
Santa Barbara Wine Country Half-Marathon	www.runsantaynez.com	13.1	May	50–71°F	Santa Ynez, CA

Name	Website	Mileage	Month	Temperature	Location
XTERRA Boordy Vineyards Scramble 5K	www.xterraplanet.com	3.1	August	71–89°F	Hydes, MD
Wineglass Marathon	www.wineglassmarathon.com	26.2	October	38–61°F	Corning, NY
The "Original" Bare Buns Fun Run	www.kaniksufamily.com	3.1	July	49–85°F	Loon Lake, WA
GIVE PEACE A CHANCE					
Continental Airlines International Friendship Run	www.ingnycmarathon.org	2.5	November	42–54°F	New York, NY
In Flanders Fields Marathon	www.marathon.be/nl/	26.2	September	56–65°F	Flanders, Belgium
Other Races in Remembrance:					
Košice Peace Marathon	www.kosicemarathon.com/en	26.2 13.1 2.6	October	37–57°F	Košice Slovakia
International Peace Marathon of Kigali	www.kigalimarathon.com	26.2 13.1 3.1	May	66–73°F	Kigali, Rwanda
The Tunnel to Towers Run	www.tunneltotowersrun.org	3.1	September	61–76°F	New York, NY

Name	Website	Mileage	Month	Temperature	Location
HIT THE BEACH					
ING Bay to Breakers	www.ingbaytobreakers.com	7.5	May	51–65°F	San Francisco, CA
Manly Wharf Hotel Soft Sand Classic	www.manlylsc.com	13 5.6 1	June	51–64°F	Manly, Australia
The Sun-Herald City2Surf	http://city2surf.sunherald.com.au	8.7	August	50–65°F	Sydney, Australia
Tahiti Moorea Marathon	www.mooreaevents.org	26.2 13.1 3.1	February	76–88°F	Moorea Island, French Polynesia
Other Beach Races: **Rio Marathon & Half-Marathon**	www.maratonadorio.com.br	26.2 13.1	June	64–75°F	Rio de Janiero, Brazil

Name	Website	Mileage	Month	Temperature	Location
LISTEN TO THE MUSIC					
Country Music Marathon & Half-Marathon	www.cmmarathon.com	26.2 13.1	April	47–70°F	Nashville, TN
Maratona delle Terre Verdiane (Verdi's Marathon)	www.verdimarathon.it	26.2 19.1 14 6.2	February	30–47°F	Salsomaggiore Terme, Italy
Reggae Marathon & Half-Marathon	www.reggaemarathon.com	26.2 13.1 6.2	December	73–85°F	Negril, Jamaica
Rock 'N' Roll Marathon Heavy Medal Series					
P.F. Chang's Rock 'N' Roll Arizona	www.rnraz.com	26.2 13.1	January	40–65°F	Phoenix, Scottsdale, and Tempe, AZ
Rock 'N' Roll Half-Marathon	www.rnrvb.com	13.1	August/September	70–78°F	Virginia Beach, VA
Rock 'N' Roll Marathon	www.rnrmarathon.com	26.2	May/June	60–73°F	San Diego, CA
Rock 'N' Roll San Antonio Marathon & Half-Marathon	www.rnrsa.com	26.2 13.1	November	50–70°F	San Antonio, TX
Rock 'N' Roll Half-Marathon San Jose	www.rnrsj.com	13.1	October	54–78°F	San Jose, CA

Name	Website	Mileage	Month	Temperature	Location
Other Rock 'N' Roll Races					
Rock 'N' Roll Seattle	www.rnrseattle.com	26.2 13.1	June	52–69°F	Seattle, WA
Rock 'N' Roll Chicago	www.rnrchicago.com	13.1	August	65–83°F	Chicago, IL
RUNNING WILD					
The Big Five Marathon®	www.big-five-marathon.com	26.2 13.1	June	45–72°F	Entabeni Game Reserve, South Africa
Other Safari Races:					
Victoria Falls Marathon	www.vicfallsmarathon.com	26.2 13.1	August	47–82°F	Victoria Falls, Zimbabwe
Burro Days "World Championship" Pack Burro Race	www.burrodays.com	29 15	July	39–65°F	Fairplay, CO
Other Colorado Pack Burro Races	www.packburroracing.com	1 to 22	May–September	35–78°F	Georgetown, Idaho Springs, Leadville, Buena Vista, Harrison, CO

Name	Website	Mileage	Month	Temperature	Location
Gorilla Runs					
Denver Gorilla Run	www.denvergorillarun.com	3.5	October	33–68°F	Denver, CO
The Great Gorilla Run	www.greatgorillas.org	4.3	September	56–67°F	London, England
New York Road Runners Empire State Building Run-Up	www.esbnyc.com/tourism/tourism_specialevents_runup.cfm	1,576 steps (86 Flights)	February	28–41°F	New York, NY
Other International Climbing Events: *More than 100 races linvolving stairs*	www.towerrunning.com	various			Various International locations
SPIRITUAL EXPERIENCES					
Big Sur International Marathon	www.bsim.org	26.2 21 10.6 9 3.1	April	53–68°F	Big Sur, CA
Additional Big Sur Races: **Big Sur Half-Marathon on Monterey Bay**	www.bigsurhalfmarathon.com	13.1 10 3.1	November	43–68°F	Monterey Bay, CA

Name	Website	Mileage	Month	Temperature	Location
Other Redwood Tree Races:					
Avenue of the Giants Marathon	www.theave.org	26.2 13.1 6.2	May	48–68°F	Humboldt Redwoods State Park, CA
Humboldt Redwoods Marathon	www.RedwoodsMarathon.org	26.2 13.1 6.2	October	48–74°F	Humboldt Redwoods State Park, CA
Everest Marathon	www.everestmarathon.org.uk	26.2	November/ December	4–46°F	Gorak Shep, Nepal
Other Everest Races:					
Tenzing-Hillary Marathon	www.everestmarathon.com	26.2 13.1	May/June	23–68°F	Everest Base Camp, Nepal
Great Ocean Road International Marathon	www.greatoceanroadmarathon.com.au	28 14.3 8.7 4	May	40–70°F	Lorne, Australia
Inca Trail to Machu Picchu	www.andesadventures.com	27.5	May/June/ August	33–68°F	Inca Trail, Cusco, Peru
Self-Transcendence Marathon	www.srichinmoyraces.org/us/races	26.2	August	61–82°F	Rockland State Park, NY

Name	Website	Mileage	Month	Temperature	Location
SWEET!					
CIGNA Falmouth Road Race	www.falmouthroadrace.com	7	August	62–78°F	Falmouth, MA
Covered Bridges Half-Marathon	www.cthm.com	13.1	June	52–77°F	Woodstock, VT
Other Covered Bridges Races:					
Annual Covered Bridge Classic	www.cbcroadrace.com	10	October	43–65°F	Atglen, PA
Swanzey Covered Bridges Half-Marathon	www.active.com	3.1 1 13.1	August/ September	56–74°F	Swanzey, NH
Credit Union Cherry Blossom Ten-Mile Run	www.cherryblossom.org	10 3.1	April	42–66°F	Washington, DC
Other Blossoming Races:					
Apple Blossom Half-Marathon	www.carpenternaturecenter.org/ appleblossom	13.1 6.2 3.1	May	47–69°F	Hastings, MN
Apple Blossom SunTrust 10K	www.thebloom.com	6.2	May	51–75°F	Winchester, VA
Cherry Blossom Marathon	www.cherryblossommarathon.com	26.2 13.1 3.1	March	44–68°F	Macon, GA
Mountain-to-Meadows Half-Marathon	www.RunLoloFess.org	13.1 3.1	June	46–74°F	Idaho/ Missoula, Montana

Name	Website	Mileage	Month	Temperature	Location
Fleet Week Half-Marathon	www.discovermwr.com/fleetweekhalf/fwhm.html	13.1	October	53–69°F	Norfolk, VA
The Other Half	www.moabhalfmarathon.org	13.1	October	38–70°F	Moab, UT
Other Red Rock Races: **Canyonlands Half-Marathon**	www.moabhalfmarathon.org	13.1	March	31–61°F	Moab, UT
Garden of the Gods 10-Mile Run	www.gardentenmile.com	10	June	50–79°F	Manitou Springs, CO
St. George Marathon	www.StGeorgemarathon.com	26.2 2.1	October	46–81°F	St. George, UT
Valley of Fire Marathon	www.vofmarathon.ning.com	26.2 13.1 6.2	November	44–66°F	Las Vegas, NV
TEAM SPORT					
Running Relays					
Klondike Trail of '98 International Road Relay	www.klondikeroadrelay.com	110-mile relay	September	44–47°F	Skagway, AL to Whitehorse, Canada
Myomed Ragnar Relay Northwest Passage	www.ragnarrelay.com/northwestpassage/index.php	187-mile relay	July	50–70°F	Blaine to Langley, WA

Name	Website	Mileage	Month	Temperature	Location
Additional Ragnar Relays	www.ragnarrelay.com				
Arizona, Boston, Florida, Los Angeles, Louisville, New York, St. Louis, Texas, Utah, Washington, DC, Wisconsin/Minnesota					
Nike Hood to Coast Relay	www.hoodtocoast.com	197-mile relay	August	42–79°F	Mount Hood to Seaside, OR
Other Relay Run Adventures:					
American Odyssey	www.AmericanOdysseyRelay.com	200-mile relay	April	33–66°F	Gettysburg, PA to Washington, DC
Reach the Beach Relay	www.rtbrelay.com	200-mile relay	September	44–73°F	Franconia to Hampton Beach, NH
Wild West Relay	www.wildwestrelay.com	195-mile relay	August	41–84°F	Fort Collins to Steamboat Springs, CO
Stadium Runs					
Brewers Charities 5K Sausage Run/Walk	www.milwaukee.brewers.mlb.com	3.1	July	63–80°F	Milwaukee, WI
Draft Day 5K	www.oymp.net	3.1	April	42–58°F	East Rutherford, NJ

Name	Website	Mileage	Month	Temperature	Location
Other Stadium Races:					
The Gupton Dodge Tom King Classic Half-Marathon	www.tomkingclassic.com	13.1 3.1 1.9	March	39–60°F	Nashville, TN
Race to Wrigley 5K Run	http://chicago.cubs.mlb.com	3.1	April	40–59°F	Chicago, IL
Obstacle Courses					
Big Sur Mud Run	www.bigsurmudrun.org	5.2	March	46–67°F	Seaside, CA
Men's Health Urbanathlon™	www.menshealthurbanathlon.com	10.5	October	46–64°F	Chicago, IL
Men's Health Urbanathlon™	www.menshealthurbanathlon.com	8.1	September	62–76°F	New York, NY
TOURIST ATTRACTIONS					
Angkor Wat Marathon	www.kathyloperevents.com/angkorwat www.angkormarathon.org	26.2 13.1 6.2 3.1	November/December	70–86°F	Angkor Wat, Cambodia
Great Wall Marathon	www.greatwall-marathon.com	26.2 13.1 6.2	September	57–78°F	Jin Shan Lin, China
Other Great Wall Races:					
Great Wall Marathon	www.great-wall-marathon.com	26.2 13.1 6.2 3.1	May	56–82°F	Tianjin Province, China

Name	Website	Mileage	Month	Temperature	Location
Intercontinental Istanbul Eurasia Marathon	www.istanbulmarathon.org	26.2 9.3	October	56–67°F	Istanbul, Turkey
The International Marathon of Marrakech	www.marathon-marrakech.com	26.2 13.1	January	44–65°F	Marrakech, Morocco
Other Exotic Races: **Standard Chartered Dubai Marathon**	www.dubaimarathon.org	26.2 6.2 1.8	January	58–75°F	Dubai, United Arab Emirates
Marabana Havana Marathon	www.cubaitours.com/marabana/running.html www.cubastartravel.com	26.2 13.1 6.2 3.1	November	72–81°F	Havana, Cuba
Three Countries Marathon	www.sparkasse-marathon.com	26.2 13.1 7.1	October/ November	46–56°F	Lindau, Germany, to Bregenz, Austria, to St. Margrethen, Switzerland
Other Multi-Country Marathons: **Marathon de Monaco et des Riviera**	www.monaco-marathon.com	26.2 6.2	November	46–59°F	Monaco to Cap Martin, France, to Latte, Italy

About the Author

KIMI PUNTILLO is a two-time Guinness Book World Record holder, a lecturer, and a journalist whose work has appeared in the *New York Times*, the *Wall Street Journal*, and *Forbes*, on NPR, and in other media. When not adventure running, she lives in New York City with her yellow Lab, Beethoven.